Praise f

Completel

lead book in the Loving Jesus w......

"Soulful and engaging."

—PUBLISHER'S WEEKLY

"Shannon Ethridge's life exhibits God's transforming power. Her response to tragedy will guide others who struggle through dark valleys, to find the light of hope that is in Christ."

—MAX LUCADO, best-selling author

"When the worst has happened, only time can bring perspective and turn trauma into triumph. Shannon Ethridge is an incredible woman who has a story to tell and a passion to share. Through experiences that would level most, she has risen as a lover of Jesus who can speak to the heart of every woman. *Completely His* calls even the most timid or scarred to a place of deep, sweet relationship with the One who patiently waits for His beloved to lean in and trust Him. I loved the book. I love Shannon's heart."

—JAN SILVIOUS, author of *Foolproofing Your Life* and *Big Girls Don't Whine*

"Insightful and daring, *Completely His* so challenged me to look at myself honestly and ask 'Am I *all* yours, God?' Shannon is completely vulnerable as she shares a longing for God in every area of her life and a step-by-step example of how to walk with Him in all aspects of daily living. This message is encouraging, life changing, and much needed by every one of us."

—SHAUNTI FELDHAHN, best-selling author of *For Women Only* and *For Men Only*

Other Books by Shannon Ethridge

Completely His
Completely Loved
Completely Forgiven
Completely Blessed
Every Woman's Battle
Every Woman's Battle Workbook
Every Young Woman's Battle
Every Young Woman's Battle Workbook
Every Single Woman's Battle
Every Woman, Every Day
Every Woman's Battle Promise Book
Preparing Your Daughter for Every Woman's Battle
Every Woman's Marriage
Every Woman's Marriage Workbook
Words of Wisdom for Women at the Well
Words of Wisdom for Well Women

LOVING JESUS
A 30-DAY GUIDE
WITHOUT LIMITS

COMPLETELY
Irresistible

Drawing Others to God's Extravagant Love

SHANNON ETHRIDGE

Best-selling author of the Every Woman's Battle series

WATERBROOK
PRESS

COMPLETELY IRRESISTIBLE
PUBLISHED BY WATERBROOK PRESS
12265 Oracle Boulevard, Suite 200
Colorado Springs, Colorado 80921
A division of Random House Inc.

All Scripture quotations, unless otherwise indicated, are taken from the Holy Bible, New Living Translation, copyright © 1996. Used by permission of Tyndale House Publishers Inc., Wheaton, Illinois 60189. All rights reserved. Scripture quotations marked (NIV) are taken from the Holy Bible, New International Version®. NIV®. Copyright © 1973, 1978, 1984 by International Bible Society. Used by permission of Zondervan Publishing House. All rights reserved.

Italics in Scripture quotations indicate the author's added emphasis.

Details in some anecdotes and stories have been changed to protect the identities of the persons involved.

ISBN 978-1-4000-7115-9

Library of Congress Cataloging-in-Publication Data
Ethridge, Shannon.
    Completely irresistible : drawing others to God's extravagant love / Shannon Ethridge.—
1st ed.p. cm. Includes bibliographical references and index.
    ISBN 978-1-4000-7115-9
    1. Witness bearing (Christianity) 2. Evangelistic work. I. Title.
    BV4520.E85 2007
    248'.5—dc22
                                                2007019146

Printed in the United States of America
2007—First Edition

10 9 8 7 6 5 4 3 2 1

SPECIAL SALES
Most WaterBrook Multnomah books are available in special quantity discounts when purchased in bulk by corporations, organizations, and special interest groups. Custom imprinting or excerpting can also be done to fit special needs. For information, please e-mail SpecialMarkets@WaterBrookPress.com or call 1-800-603-7051.

CONTENTS

An Invitation to Share
God's Awesome Mission

*G*od loves us so much that He sent His Son, Jesus, to live among us and then die for us so that we could be reconciled with God. Jesus accomplished this mission, yet not all have received this memo or believed this news. Consequently, we've been invited to help spread the word throughout the world about God's extravagant love, for His deepest desire is that everyone be saved (John 3:16). While this charge may seem overwhelming, it's actually a delightful opportunity—similar to when a bride gets to toss her bouquet to others who long to experience the love she has found in her groom.

Have you ever witnessed a bride tossing her bouquet at a wedding reception? It's an irresistible invitation because the tradition holds an irresistible promise. Young women get all giddy as they eagerly flock around the bride, hoping to soon become the next in line at the bridal shop. The newlywed flings her flowers into the air. All the girls squeal, scramble, and stretch to grab them. But only one lucky lady walks away from that experience holding fresh flowers in her arms, stars in her eyes, and hope in her heart that she will soon meet her own true love.

You and I have an even more compelling invitation to extend to others— the invitation to become a part of the bride of Christ; and this invitation isn't limited to one person, but is open to all who'll receive it. What if our lives were so spiritually irresistible that others were naturally drawn toward us, hoping to experience the extravagant love that we've discovered ourselves? How easy it would be to carry out the mission that our heavenly Bridegroom has entrusted to us!

If this sounds appealing to you, then you are holding the right book. Welcome to *Completely Irresistible*, the last devotional book in a series of four that follow the lead book in the series, *Completely His: Loving Jesus Without Limits*. If you've not yet read it or the first three devotionals, I encourage you to do so to ensure that you receive the most from the series. However, doing so isn't a prerequisite in order for you to glean great things from this one.

Each devotional is designed to deepen your commitment to your heavenly Bridegroom, Jesus Christ, and to help you embrace your role as His beloved bride. Through thirty days of intimate time in God's Word, you'll discover:

- how far God has gone to reveal Himself to us and draw us closer (the focus of *Completely Loved: Recognizing God's Passionate Pursuit of Us*)
- how God can use you mightily in spite of your shortcomings (the message in *Completely Forgiven: Responding to God's Transforming Grace*)
- how God lavishes both His presence and His presents upon us (the theme of *Completely Blessed: Discovering God's Extraordinary Gifts*)
- how our love for God cannot be contained and can be shared naturally (the emphasis of this devotional)

Just in case you didn't catch that last part, let me draw your attention to it. Sharing God's extravagant love with the world isn't something we have to strive for and stress over. It can be done naturally. In fact, it can become second nature, like breathing.

Over these next thirty days, we'll consider how you can spontaneously share your spiritual gifts and maximize your opportunities to draw others into a love relationship with Christ. We'll examine the potential impact of swimming against the tide, turning misery into ministry, and sparking a revolution in this world. You'll recognize the evangelistic benefits of simple things, such as making time for others, showing hospitality, and modeling integrity. You'll be encouraged to bridge cultural gaps, love without fear, and focus on what matters most. By the time you get to the end of this book, I believe you'll see yourself in a completely different light—recognizing that you are more naturally cut out for bringing others to Jesus than you previously thought.

I'm so glad you've chosen to join me on yet another thirty-day journey! Get ready to discover and celebrate some of the natural evangelistic talents that your Creator has already woven into the fibers of your being, and recognize how God might want to use *you* to draw others toward His extravagant love.

GO FISH!

Daily reading: Matthew 4:18–25

Key passage: One day as Jesus was walking along the shore beside the Sea of Galilee, he saw two brothers—Simon, also called Peter, and Andrew— fishing with a net, for they were commercial fishermen. Jesus called out to them, "Come, be my disciples, and I will show you how to fish for people!" And they left their nets at once and went with him. (Matthew 4:18–20)

---

*G*reg and I had been dating for several months, and he asked to take me somewhere special for my birthday. *He's going to propose,* I suspected. *I'm getting an engagement ring for my birthday!* Christmas was just around the corner, and I had already bought him a camcorder and placed it under my tree. I decided to give it to him early so we'd have it for the trip. *We'll be able to get his proposal on video!*

My birthday arrived, and we sat in Greg's Ford Bronco by Broken Bow Lake. "May I give you your birthday present now?" he asked.

"No! I have to give you your Christmas present first!" I insisted. He opened the camcorder and was delighted with his new, high-tech toy. We played with it long enough to figure out how it worked, then I caught his cute face on camera as he repeated, "May I give you your present *now?*"

"YES!" I exclaimed. He reached behind the seat and brought out a brand-new...*rod and reel*! I couldn't believe it. He gave me a fishing pole for my birthday! Greg rambled on all afternoon in that tipsy canoe about his fishing adventures, how much he loved the sport, and how glad he was to have a girlfriend who was willing to fish alongside him. I kept thinking of things I'd rather be doing—like getting engaged!

A few men in Jesus' day also loved to fish, but Jesus had something else in mind. "Follow me...and I will make you fishers of men," He urged Peter, Andrew, James, and John (Mark 1:17, NIV). They didn't argue. They dropped their nets, abandoned their boats, and dedicated their lives to the highest of callings: to draw others into a relationship with Christ.

Chances are, you've come to know Christ because someone fished for your soul, whether it was a parent, preacher, teacher, or friend. Are you willing to do the same?

Perhaps you're thinking, *Well, evangelism is not really my thing.*

God has often called people to do things that were uncomfortable for them...that weren't their "thing." And if these people had let their discomfort stop them from doing what God had asked, we would all be without hope. Think about it. What if Noah had said, "Building boats isn't really my thing"? Not one person would have survived the flood, and the human race would have been terminated right then and there. What if David had insisted, "Writing psalms is not really my thing"? Millions of people would have missed out on some of the most comforting poetry ever written. What if Mary had replied to the angel, "Virgin births aren't really my thing"? She would have missed out on an unequaled opportunity to serve God and humankind. What if Jesus had said, "Crosses aren't really My thing"? We would be doomed, both now and forever.

Life is about much more than simply doing our own thing. We can live for a much higher purpose—God's thing, drawing people to Himself. Our heavenly Bridegroom seeks a bride who will go fishing for souls alongside Him.

Let's reflect for a moment on how God likely feels when we refuse to go fishing with Him. Imagine your husband walking you down the aisle, placing a wedding band on your finger, committing his life to you, and providing abundantly for your every need. Yet, instead of proudly proclaiming to be his wife and striving to be his helpmate, you decide to go incognito on the whole marriage thing. You keep your maiden name and refuse to wear a wedding band because you don't want others to know you are married. You choose not to talk about your husband or your life together for fear that someone might discover your secret. You fail to listen to your husband when he expresses his most pressing needs for your assistance. How will he feel about your commitment to him? Not so convinced of your all-consuming love, right? Right.

God feels the same way when we choose to be incognito Christians. If we hide our relationship with Him and ignore His desire for us to be "fishers of men" because we're too embarrassed to be evangelists, how will He feel about our commitment to Him? Actually, we don't have to answer that question. Jesus already did in Luke 9:23–26:

> Then he said to the crowd, "If any of you wants to be my follower,
> you must put aside your selfish ambition, shoulder your cross daily,
> and follow me. If you try to keep your life for yourself, you will lose
> it. But if you give up your life for me, you will find true life. And how
> do you benefit if you gain the whole world but lose or forfeit your
> own soul in the process? *If a person is ashamed of me and my message,
> I, the Son of Man, will be ashamed of that person when I return in my
> glory and in the glory of the Father and the holy angels.*"

The idea of our heavenly Bridegroom being ashamed of us when He returns is almost too painful to think about. If we are ashamed of Jesus, we must question the authenticity of our relationship. But if we are not ashamed of Christ and want to share His love with others, Scripture says Jesus will not be ashamed to call us His brothers and sisters (Hebrews 2:11), and that God is not ashamed to be our God (Hebrews 11:16).

Perhaps the idea of knocking on doors to invite people to church or passing out tracts on street corners doesn't appeal to you. That's okay. There are far more effective means of inviting others to experience God's love. We're going to discuss many of those ways in this book. If you are ready to more naturally and effectively draw others toward God's extravagant love, then read on to find out more about how you can live a completely irresistible life.

HOLDING HIS HAND

Ideally, how many people would I like to take to heaven with me someday? Who, in particular, are some of those individuals or groups of people?

_____

_____

Do I care enough for these people to allow God to draw me out of my comfort zone and make me a "fisher of men"? Why or why not?

_____

_____

If evangelism came far more naturally to me, how might other people be affected? How might their lives change for the better?

_____

_____

> *Magnificent Holy Father,*
>
> *We rejoice over the fact that You are never ashamed to be called our God, and we sincerely hope we are never ashamed to be called the bride of Christ. Open our eyes to the vision You had in mind when You called us to be "fishers of men," and give us a heart to naturally draw others toward You. In Jesus' name. Amen.*

TELL YOUR STORY

Daily reading: Luke 8:1–3; John 19:17–20:18

Key passage: Mary Magdalene found the disciples and told them, "I have seen the Lord!" Then she gave them his message. (John 20:18)

---

*I*f there's a biblical character with whom I'd like to sit around the campfire, it's Mary Magdalene. Could you imagine the marvelous stories she could tell? Stories about what it's like to be possessed by seven demons, and how she felt after Jesus drove them from her…stories about how she was part of a group of women who followed Jesus around, caring for His needs…stories about the silly things the disciples did as they jockeyed for position and tried to perform mighty miracles. But the story I'd be most interested to hear? What it was like to be the first person Jesus appeared to after His resurrection. Surely the other disciples got goose bumps as Mary told them *that* story.

Is anything more powerful, or more memorable, than a good story? I think not. Our earliest childhood memories are marked by classic stories such as *Cinderella, Jack and the Beanstalk,* and *Aesop's Fables.* Our first understanding of God most likely came through great Old Testament stories such as Noah's ark, David and Goliath, and Daniel in the lions' den. The gospel writers paint a picture of who Jesus is by telling all kinds of wonderful stories—stories about His miracles, stories about His ministry, and stories about the stories Jesus Himself told (the parables). Yes, Jesus knew the power of a good story.

Author Barbara Hardy insightfully proclaimed, "We dream in narrative, daydream in narrative, remember, anticipate, hope, despair, believe, doubt, plan, revise, criticize, gossip, learn, hate and live by narrative."[1] Stories shape our world and stir us mentally, emotionally, and spiritually. That's why well-crafted novels sell millions of copies. It's why we get hooked into watching a one-hour television program after watching the first two minutes. It's why we spend billions of dollars each year at the box office to see movies. No one can resist a great story.

And of course, the greatest story of all time is that of God sending His Son to earth in the form of a man to redeem fallen humanity. That's why the Bible is the best-selling book of all time. The story of how humanity responds to God's passionate pursuit of us can be equally as awe-inspiring. As believers in Christ, we have the power to eternally impact others simply by sharing God's story, as well as our own.

President Jimmy Carter could tell many wonderful stories, but one he shares in *Sources of Strength: Meditations on Scripture for a Living Faith* will always stick with me. Three men were invited to give a five-minute speech to 17,000 delegates at the Southern Baptist Convention: Carter, Billy Graham, and a truck driver. The eloquent Dr. Graham spoke first, Carter spoke last, and sandwiched in between these two great men was an uneducated truck driver who had never given a speech in his life. The truck driver confessed he didn't think he'd live through the nerve-wracking experience. Yet after Graham delivered his powerful message, the truck driver slowly approached the microphone. He mumbled, "I was always drunk, and didn't have any friends. The only people I knew were men like me who hung around the bars in the town where I lived."

He went on to say that someone came along and told him about Christ, and he became a believer and wanted to tell others about the Lord. He studied the Bible with some Christian men and prepared to witness to people.

Since he felt comfortable in barrooms, he decided to talk to people there. The bartender wasn't sympathetic, telling the new convert he was bad for business and a nuisance.

Not discouraged, the truck driver kept on with his mission, and in time the people at the bar began asking questions. He said, "At first they treated me like a joke, but I kept up with the questions and when I couldn't answer one, I went and got the answer and came back with it. Fourteen of my friends became Christians."[2]

Fourteen people! If this truck driver's story about what Christ did for him convinced fourteen barroom buddies to accept Jesus as Lord and Savior, surely God can make an evangelist out of anyone. Even you.

Jimmy Carter goes on to say, "The truck driver's speech, of course, was the highlight of the convention. I don't believe anyone who was there will ever forget that five-minute fumbling statement—or remember what I or even Billy Graham had to say."[3] In other words, it's not our status or our eloquence that give us success in our evangelistic efforts. It's about our sincerity and how well we bring glory to God.

Perhaps you are thinking, *But my testimony isn't all that dramatic!* As I explained in *Completely His*, it doesn't have to be. Still, many people feel that for their testimony to be contagious, they need to have a dramatic conversion experience. My daughter used to feel this way. At eleven years old, she was preparing for a mission trip to Costa Rica and had to put her testimony in writing. She confessed, "Mom, I think my salvation story is pretty boring. Sometimes I'm tempted to go out and do something bad just so I'll have a more powerful testimony."

My response was a mixture of panic and sympathy. I assured Erin that it's okay to simply say, "I thank God that He made His presence known to me before I made a total mess of my life." Such a story is a powerful testimony of how He sovereignly protects us from ourselves when we are willing to submit to His lordship.

So what's your story? Like the truck driver and my daughter, have you taken time to prepare it and practice it? Are you willing to share it with others? I encourage you to do so. As you share your story of what Christ has done for you, you'll be inviting others to share in His unconditional love as well.

HOLDING HIS HAND

Why do stories appeal to people? Do they appeal to me? If so, why?

_____

_____

_____

Should the story of God sending His Son to save us from our sins appeal to those who are lost in their sin? Does the story bear repeating? Why or why not?

_____

_____

_____

What might the Holy Spirit do through me if I rehearse my life's story and make myself available to share it with others?

_____

_____

_____

Magnificent Holy Father,

There is no greater story than the one You reveal to us in Your Word! Give us the courage and creativity to reveal that story to others so that they may also dwell in the house of the Lord forever. In Jesus' most holy and precious name. Amen.

STAND STRONG IN THE FACE OF PERSECUTION

Daily reading: Acts 6:8–7:60

Key passage: But Stephen, full of the Holy Spirit, gazed steadily upward into heaven and saw the glory of God, and he saw Jesus standing in the place of honor at God's right hand.... And as they stoned him, Stephen prayed, "Lord Jesus, receive my spirit." And he fell to his knees, shouting, "Lord, don't charge them with this sin!" And with that, he died. (Acts 7:55, 59–60)

*A*s odd as it sounds, one of my favorite places to walk is a cemetery. I once heard a speaker say that a cemetery isn't just a place where bodies are buried, but a place where dreams are buried as well. Many people go to their graves without ever seeing their dreams come to life or fulfilling the purpose for which God created them. As I look at the names and dates on tombstones, I can't help but wonder, *Did these people take their dreams with them to their graves, or did they see them fulfilled?* It's a time of deep reflection for me as I contemplate, *Am I doing all that I can to fulfill every dream God has for my life?*

Whenever I walk through the local cemetery here in Garden Valley, Texas, I always stroll over to one of my favorite markers—that of evangelist Leonard Ravenhill where these words are carved in granite: IS WHAT YOU ARE LIVING FOR WORTH CHRIST DYING FOR?

Many people throughout church history could say yes to this question. You read about one of them in today's Scripture reading. Stephen firmly believed that Jesus was the long-awaited Messiah the Jews had been hoping for. He was so convicted by this belief that no angry glares, violent threats, or even hard rocks hurled at his head could convince him to renounce his belief.

As you read the account of Stephen, you may have had flashbacks to Jesus' trial and torture. Indeed, just a few years before, Jesus stood before this very court claiming His authority as Messiah. In Mark 14:61–62, we read Jesus' reply after He was accused of blasphemy:

> Then the high priest asked him, "Are you the Messiah, the Son of the blessed God?"
>
> Jesus said, "I am, and you will see me, the Son of Man, sitting at God's right hand in the place of power and coming back on the clouds of heaven."

Surely Jesus' words came back to haunt some of the members of this council as Stephen, at the close of his discourse, gazed heavenward and proclaimed, "Look, I see the heavens opened and the Son of Man standing in the place of honor at God's right hand!" (Acts 7:56). In other words, "Hey! What Jesus was trying to tell you about Himself was the truth, guys! He's taken His rightful place next to God in heaven! You crucified your Messiah!"

How did his listeners respond to Stephen's proclamation? They covered their ears and shouted over his voice so they wouldn't have to hear the truth. Their hearts were hardened, so much so that they didn't mind silencing Stephen with a brutal beating that would send him to his death. As Stephen was being stoned, his final words are also reminiscent of Jesus' as he pleaded, "Lord, don't charge them with this sin!" (comparing Acts 7:60 with Luke 23:34). What an incredibly loving thing to say about your enemies as they are killing you!

While it is extremely rare for Christians to be killed today simply for sharing their faith, persecution often takes other forms. There are missionaries, pastors, and evangelists sitting in jail cells in foreign countries, such as China and Indonesia, for no other crime than sharing their faith in Christ. (Learn about these prisoners and how you can pray for them or even write to them by visiting the Voice of the Martyrs Web site at www.persecution.com.) Even here in the land of religious freedom, we may find ourselves in places or situations where we face persecution. If God called you to share your testimony in an inner-city homeless shelter, outside a brothel in Las Vegas, or at a women's prison or a juvenile detention center where you knew the residents would mock you and hurl insults at you, would you be obedient to that call? Would you be able to muster up enough courage to stand strong in the face of persecution? In a worst-case scenario, would you be able to stare down the barrel of a gun held by a hostile atheist and cling to your confession that Jesus Christ is your Lord and Savior?

I pray none of us ever face such a test, but surely if we had to make the choice, we'd rather die proclaiming our belief in God than to live with the realization that we'd denied Him.

I'm so thankful for the examples of martyrs such as Stephen and some of the other disciples. Let's emulate their rock-solid faith, both in life and someday in death, particularly if we're ever faced with the choice they had to make. Let's live by the life-changing truth that death isn't the worst thing that can happen to a person. Eternal separation from God is.

Living for Christ is indeed worth dying for. May we always be willing to boldly proclaim our faith in Jesus, both as we walk through life and as we knock on death's door someday. Such a testimony will surely inspire others to love our God with all their heart, mind, soul, and strength as well.

HOLDING HIS HAND

Have I ever been persecuted for my faith? How did I respond? How did I feel about my response?

_____

_____

_____

Is there anything or anyone that could convince me to forsake my God? Why or why not?

_____

_____

_____

How could my remaining faithful to Christ, even in the face of persecution, inspire others to place their trust in God as well?

_____

_____

_____

Lord Jesus,

Thank You that when faced with the decision to either save us or save Yourself, You chose to save us. Give us the same resolve to withstand persecution and even die for You if necessary, so that we can show the world that what we are living for is indeed worth dying for. In Jesus' name. Amen.

GO WHERE GOD SENDS

Daily reading: Acts 9:1–31

Key passage: "But Lord," exclaimed Ananias, "I've heard about the terrible things this man has done to the believers in Jerusalem! And we hear that he is authorized by the leading priests to arrest every believer in Damascus."

But the Lord said, "Go and do what I say. For Saul is my chosen instrument to take my message to the Gentiles and to kings, as well as to the people of Israel." (Acts 9:13–15)

---

*W*esley Autrey, a fifty-year-old construction worker, entered a New York City subway station with his two daughters the first week of 2007. There he witnessed a startling scene.

Nineteen-year-old Cameron Hollopeter was suffering a seizure while waiting for a train. He fell from the platform onto the tracks just as an inbound train was approaching. Autrey realized that everyone else who witnessed the scene was frozen in fear, so he decided to go where no one else dared—onto the tracks to grab hold of the boy.

Autrey rolled the teen and himself into a drainage trough cut between the two tracks. Seconds later the train thundered over them with only inches to spare. Miraculously, neither suffered injuries.

This new Hero of Harlem has received lots of media attention and gratitude from city officials, including the city's highest award for civic achievement and a $10,000 reward from Donald Trump. Autrey was quoted as responding, "Good things happen when you do good."[1]

In today's Scripture passage you read about another man who did something good—Ananias. While I don't know what good things happened to Ananias as a result of his obedience to God, I know that I am a direct beneficiary of his brave act. If you've gleaned any wisdom from the letters Paul wrote to the New Testament churches, then you are a beneficiary of Ananias's bravery as well.

Put yourself in his position for a moment. There's a guy in town who is infamous for his hatred of all followers of Christ (you included). He was one of the official witnesses at the stoning of Stephen (Acts 8:1). He reportedly utters "threats with every breath" (Acts 9:1), and is so eager to destroy Christians that he recently requested permission from the high priest to go throughout the region putting believers in chains. Your freedom and life are in jeopardy because of this madman.

Then God tells you to go to this murderer and remove his physical and spiritual blindness! Hello? And why don't you walk into this hungry lion's cage and pull the splinter from his paw while you are at it? Ananias's obedience in going over to Straight Street and witnessing to Saul was no small act. It took more than a lion's share of courage. How did he get so bravehearted? He knew God personally and intimately. He trusted God completely. He feared disobeying his Lord more than he feared what Saul might do to him.

Because of Ananias's faithfulness, Saul saw the light, both literally and figuratively. Now called Paul, he became even more impassioned for spreading the good news of the gospel of Christ than he was about destroying it. Thanks to the passionate letters he penned by the inspiration of the Holy Spirit, we can hold God's heart for His New Testament church in our hands and read it every day.

Sometimes I wonder if Ananias had any idea what ripple effects his courage would have on the body of Christ. Sometimes I wonder if *we* have any idea what ripple effects *our* courage could have on the body of Christ.

To illustrate your evangelistic potential in the simplest of terms, let's consider the popular shampoo commercial of the 1970s and 1980s. A beautiful blond woman says, "You'll love your hair so much that you'll tell two friends, and they'll tell two friends, and so on, and so on, and so on.... All the while, faces are multiplying exponentially on the screen.

If we can love something as trivial as shampoo enough to tell two friends, surely our love for Christ should compel us to tell at least two friends. Then as they proceed to tell two friends, and so on, and so on, the body of Christ can reach its full potential. When it does, Jesus can finally come back and claim His spiritual bride, and we can dance and dine together at the wedding supper of the Lamb!

All we have to do is be willing to go where God sends us, and tell people about His extravagant love for them. The results are entirely up to Him, but the initiative is entirely up to us.

Holding His Hand

Is God calling me to do something that seems difficult or frightening? What is it and how do I feel about it? How might today's devotional affect my feelings?

Have I ever allowed fear to prevent me from spreading the gospel of Jesus Christ? What happened?

_____

_____

_____

_____

How do I view God? Do I have a proper fear (reverence, respect, awe) of Him? Why do I feel the way I do?

_____

_____

_____

_____

Most Awesome Lord,

The primary thing we should fear most in this world is the thought of living without You. The secondary thing we should fear most is the thought of others living without You. Remove our spiritual blindness, and give us the courage to lead others into the light of Your love. Amen.

EXERCISE YOUR AUTHORITY

Daily reading: Matthew 28:16–20; Galatians 1

Key passage: I [Paul] was not appointed by any group or by human authority. My call is from Jesus Christ himself and from God the Father, who raised Jesus from the dead. (Galatians 1:1)

---

*I*magine being approached on a downtown street by an elderly homeless man. His dated jacket and pants are tattered, wrinkled, and stained. He smells like the Dumpster he rummaged through for today's meager lunch. The coarse gray hair sticking out from under his toboggan cap is matted and his scruffy face reminds you of sandpaper. He walks up to you with a snaggle-toothed grin, puts his face up close to yours, looks you in the eye, and says with breath so strong it could knock you down, "I'd like to give you a million dollars!"

How would you respond? Would you hold out your hand in anticipation, or would you laugh and keep walking? Would you ask questions to find out if he's serious, or would you assume he's deluded and ignore him?

Chances are, none of us would give the man a second thought. If we did, it would be out of concern for him, not out of expectation that he could do anything that would benefit us—much less give us a million dollars.

But if a well-dressed, clean-cut man stepped out of a chauffeur-driven Rolls-Royce and approached us with the same offer, we'd be much more inclined to hear what he has to say, right? More than likely.

We are wise enough to understand this simple principle: *you can't give what you don't have.* The homeless person most likely wouldn't have a million dollars to give away, but the rich one might be able to live up to such a promise. The true test of our ability to follow through on any promise is this: Can we deliver the goods? Can we put our money where our mouth is? Are we the "real deal" or a counterfeit?

The essence of the Christian life is that we embody Christ's love, power, and forgiveness, and that we tell others about His love. Paul obviously understood this concept, as he boldly proclaimed the gospel everywhere he went. He gathered a group of co-laborers together and set sail, traveling from city to city as an ambassador for Christ. He needed no other authority than that which God had already given him.

Perhaps you are thinking that such authority comes from some sort of special commissioning. Actually, we've already received that commission, we just fail to recognize it much of the time. Check out these verses from Matthew:

> Jesus came and told his disciples, "I have been given *complete author-ity* in heaven and on earth. Therefore, [I am *giving you* this authority to] go and make disciples of all the nations, baptizing them in the name of the Father and the Son and the Holy Spirit. Teach these new disciples to obey all the commands I have given you. And be sure of this: I am with you always, even to the end of the age. (Matthew 28:18–20)

Jesus didn't intend for these words to apply strictly to the disciples who were standing there in His presence. He intended these words for *all* of His disciples for all time. How do we know? He said, "I am with you always, even to the end of the age." He wasn't implying that these disciples would live forever. Most would die within a few years. Jesus was granting His authority to all believers throughout all time, which includes you and me. If this is true, we don't have to be missionaries or on staff at a church in order to tell others the good news contained in the gospels. We don't have to be Bible teachers or youth group leaders. We just have to be Christ followers.

Think about the people you encounter on a regular basis—family, friends, co-workers, neighbors, and so on. If you were to tell them about Christ's love, how would they respond? Based on what they see in your life, would the love of God be so overwhelmingly evident that they would give 100 percent credence to what you say? Or would they consider your sales pitch to be false advertising?

Once again, we can't give what we don't have. If the people around you witness you continually walking in defeat, overwhelmed by your circumstances, submitting to sin as if you are powerless over it, discouraged, depressed, and angry with yourself and others, will they find your life attractive? Will they want what you have? Absolutely not! If you can't claim authority over your own issues, why would they think you could tell them how they might gain authority over their own?

On the other hand, if people see that you are generous, encouraged, energized, joyful in spite of any difficult circumstances, conquering temptation and resisting sin, and at peace with yourself and others, they are going to get the impression that you have something they want. And they may even ask you how to get it.

When you exercise the authority that Christ has given you, your lifestyle becomes completely irresistible to others. As you go about your daily routine, you'll be naturally tossing the bouquet to other potential brides of Christ.

They will reach out to you in an effort to find out how they can have a life like yours. When they do, you can introduce them to the Lover of their souls.

HOLDING HIS HAND

How have I treated other people in my life this past week? Have I been kind, patient, compassionate—even when others have treated me unkindly? Have I looked after the interests of others over my own interests?

_____

_____

_____

What things in my life might I need to exercise my God-given authority over in order to more successfully draw others toward Christ's extravagant love?

_____

_____

_____

Do I believe that God's commissioning is all I need to share His love with others? Why or why not?

_____

_____

_____

Lord Jesus,

You alone have complete authority over all things, and we thank You for the authority that You have already granted to us to make disciples of all nations. Inspire us to boldly proclaim the love You have for others, and help us to bask in the love You have for us as well. Amen.

SWIM AGAINST
THE TIDE

Daily reading: 1 Peter 4:1–19

Key passage: So then, since Christ suffered physical pain, you must arm yourselves with the same attitude he had, and be ready to suffer, too. For if you are willing to suffer for Christ, you have decided to stop sinning. And you won't spend the rest of your life chasing after evil desires, but you will be anxious to do the will of God. (1 Peter 4:1–2)

On a recent summer vacation to Colorado, our family seized an opportunity to fulfill a dream of mine—to go on a white-water-rafting expedition. I'd seen television commercials of white-water rafters, and it looked so invigorating. In Colorado we'd seen lots of enticing billboards and brochures for white-water rafting companies who will outfit you and guide you down the river, and it piqued my interest. We eagerly anticipated being part of the action instead of just looking at pictures of someone else experiencing the adventure.

When the day finally arrived, my adrenaline was flowing almost as fast as that river. We were fitted for life vests, briefed as to what to do in certain situations, and bused to where our nine-mile journey through Bighorn Sheep Canyon and the Royal Gorge would begin.

However, about two miles into the expedition, our raft hit a little snag— literally. Traveling at a quick rate of speed, we hit a patch of rocks that brought us to a halt, and the jolt sent my fourteen-year-old daughter flying over the edge and into the rushing water. What a nerve-racking feeling to watch your baby girl get whisked away in the current while you are stuck in a stationary position!

Fortunately, Erin encountered another rock within a short distance and clung to it until our guide was able to free us. As we cruised by, Erin grabbed hold of her dad's paddle and he hurled her up and out of the water, safely back into the boat.

At another point in the journey, we were given the opportunity to jump into the water to cool off for a while. Even though the water wasn't moving nearly as swiftly as it was when Erin fell out, it was still all I could do to not get swept away. I would dig my feet into the rocky silt beneath, but within seconds I would get dislodged by the current. I thought about trying to swim upstream to return to the boat, but I knew the chances of success were slim. So I grabbed hold of a rock, just as Erin had done. After a short time, my arms grew weary, so I decided I was cool enough. I stuck out my thumb in a hitchhiker position, and as soon as the guide paddled toward me, I returned to the safety of the boat.

Swimming against the current is incredibly difficult—both in white water and in our world. Without a rock to hold on to, we can get swept away far too easily. Even with a rock to grasp, in the midst of strong surrounding currents we can grow weary at times. I suspect Peter knew this well as he penned the words, "So if you are suffering according to God's will, keep on doing what is right, and trust yourself to the God who made you, for he will never fail you" (1 Peter 4:19). In other words, "Swimming against the tide of unrighteousness in our world is hard, but don't give up and just go with the flow! God is a steady, immovable Rock! Cling to Him!"

Not only are we to cling to God, our solid Rock, as Christians we are called to be a rock that can help others resist the pull of a sinful world. I remember looking for such a rock when I was single. Although I claimed to believe in God, I wasn't living a transformed Christian life. I had killed my conscience over and over and found myself caught up in the pull of not one, but two different premarital sexual relationships simultaneously. Neither of the men cared about my unfaithfulness, but I knew this was doubly inappropriate.

I consulted two friends about what I should do. One was a co-worker who wore a cross around her neck and attended church regularly. Her response was, "Oh, Shannon, I know lots of people who are sleeping with more than one person at a time. It's no big deal." Her advice was to just go with the flow of the world.

Fortunately, my other friend was much wiser. She encouraged me to *stop* having sex with not just one guy, but *both* of them. "It will be hard," she acknowledged, "but remember that God blesses those who suffer for the sake of righteousness." During this season I first realized just how addicted I had become to relationships to medicate my emotional pain. It was hard to resist the pull of the world, especially when I liked my sin so much. But as I let go of my inappropriate relationships and held tightly to Jesus, He began revealing Himself to me in new and unprecedented ways. I became stronger than I ever realized I could be. I developed spiritual muscles I didn't know I had. And not only was I able to swim against the cultural tide, I eventually became a rock in other people's lives, pointing the way to the ultimate Rock we have in Jesus Christ.

Guess which of the two friends is still in my life today? Yep. The second one. When we encourage people to live their best Christian life, we are being the best friend we can be. We are drawing them toward God's love instead of letting them get caught up in the flow of an ungodly world. As they cling to Him, their hunger and thirst for true love will be fulfilled.

HOLDING HIS HAND

How does my life compare to the culture around me? Do I swim against the tide, or do I often choose to just go with the flow?

_____

_____

_____

If someone is looking for spiritual stability in her life, am I a good example for her to follow? If everyone emulated my level of conviction, would this world be a better place? Why or why not?

_____

_____

_____

What might need to change in me if I am to live the kind of irresistible life that Jesus lived?

_____

_____

_____

Most Holy God,

Thank You for being the Rock we can always cling to even in the strongest of cultural currents. Your righteousness is unwavering and is forever available to us when we hold on to You with conviction. Help us swim against the tide of immorality, and show us how to help others do the same. Amen.

LEND A HELPING HAND

Daily reading: Luke 10:30–37

Key passage: "Now which of these three would you say was a neighbor to the man who was attacked by bandits?" Jesus asked.

The man replied, "The one who showed him mercy."

Then Jesus said, "Yes, now go and do the same." (Luke 10:36–37)

---

*A*lthough we associate the term *good Samaritan* with biblical times, it became evident on August 29, 2005, that many "good Samaritans" attend my church. As Hurricane Katrina's floodwaters violently crossed the levees of New Orleans, thousands of Louisiana residents scrambled across the state line, seeking refuge from the storm. Fortunately, thousands of east Texans were ready to lend a helping hand.

Although Rob and Johanna Cox have a full nest with their four home-schooled children, they made room for family members and friends—sixteen of them, some staying as long as a month. The Coxes created makeshift beds on just about every square inch of available floor space and prepared three meals a day for twenty hungry tummies from whatever was available or had been brought over by caring neighbors. Johanna stopped homeschooling for a while as her children were learning invaluable lessons about the most important things in life—loving and caring for others. Johanna says, "Four different families with different temperaments, who are all used to having their own space, lived under the same roof during this time, yet it wasn't nearly as much of a burden as it was a blessing."

The Desmond family knocked on local hotel room doors, inviting evacuees to a fellowship meal at our church, as well as inviting some into their own home for meals. They also spent hours on the Internet, using satellite photos to discover the status of the homes of the people they met. This information helped families discern whether it was safe to return to their neighborhood to salvage what they could of their possessions. The Lewis family loaned their Suburban to a New Orleans man so he could pick up vanloads of relatives from various airports. The Lewises also frequently checked in on evacuees at the local hotel to see what needs they could provide.

Other families gathered massive amounts of blankets, pillows, clothes, shoes, diapers, food, baby formula, as well as children's games, books, and crayons so that thousands of people in local area shelters could manage for several days. Some members of our congregation arranged for free haircuts, took people to get their eyeglasses replaced and prescriptions filled, and helped individuals establish new banking relationships (since some New Orleans banks were temporarily crippled). Women took other women out to lunch, just to get them out of their hotel rooms for a break. On a daily basis for many weeks, east Texans tried to anticipate every physical, spiritual, mental, and emotional need of our Louisiana neighbors and strove to meet those needs however we could.

Unfortunately, not everyone had a tender heart toward our friends in need. Some in the area voiced concerns that many of these evacuees were "undesirable" and feared that if we showed too much hospitality, some would settle in the community on a permanent basis. When I heard about this, I thought of the people in Jesus' parable who walked right on by, ignoring the needs of the suffering Jewish man.

While helping others may feel like a burden to some, to the bride of Christ, it is an enormous blessing. Just ask the Lewis family or the Desmonds or the Coxes or any other family who reached out in love to the folks of Louisiana, "Who was blessed more during this time?" They'll confirm what the Bible says in Acts 20:35, "It is more blessed to *give* than to receive," which is all the more reason to lend a helping hand whenever possible.

HOLDING HIS HAND

Is there a particular person or group of people who has a need I could fulfill? If so, who are they, and how could I lend a helping hand?

_____

_____

_____

_____

How does it make me feel when I am able to be a blessing to someone else? Who benefits more—me or the recipient of my compassion? Why?

_____

_____

_____

_____

How does God feel about the person who lends a helping hand? What blessings may await that person in heaven?

_____

_____

_____

_____

Lord Jesus,

We acknowledge that compassion doesn't come naturally in this "look out for number one" world we live in. Any tenderness we feel toward another human being is even more of a blessing to us than to others. Keep our hearts soft toward one another, and show us how we can lend a hand to make a lasting difference in people's lives. Amen.

DELIVER
GOOD NEWS

Daily reading: Romans 10:1–15

Key passage: But how can they call on him to save them unless they believe in him? And how can they believe in him if they have never heard about him? And how can they hear about him unless someone tells them? And how will anyone go and tell them without being sent? That is what the Scriptures mean when they say, "How beautiful are the feet of those who bring good news!" (Romans 10:14–15)

There are times when I really don't care to see our mailman, and there are other times when he's a welcome friend. On the days when there's nothing in my mailbox but bills and random advertisements, I don't appreciate Joe for coming by. However, on other occasions I am thrilled—such as when he delivers birthday or holiday cards from friends and family, or when he delivers my semiannual royalty check from my publisher, or when he rings the doorbell to deliver some long-awaited mail-order package from my favorite catalog company.

If it's bad news we're receiving, we often want to shoot the messenger. If it's good news, we want to hug the messenger's neck. So let me ask you this question: *why do we fear offending people by sharing the good news of the gospel message with them?*

Think about it. Can you imagine receiving better news than this?

- All of the bad stuff you've ever done in life—it's completely gone. Your slate's wiped clean. Here's a fresh new start, and more grace and mercy are available if you find yourself failing again.

- Wondering how you can exercise power over temptations that ultimately serve to bring you down? The Holy Spirit can lift you far above any temptation and make you an overcomer.

- Are you afraid of what will happen to you after you die? Here's your all-expenses-paid, one-way ticket to paradise. You'll get to reside in heavenly bliss forever.

- Wondering how to find purpose, meaning, satisfaction, and fulfillment in life until then? Here's a Bible. It's your basic instruction manual on how to discover all those things and more.

- Feeling overwhelmed by life's circumstances? Here's where you can find a sense of peace that passes all understanding.

- Ever get lonely? Let me introduce you to the Friend who will never leave you nor forsake you.

- Looking to become a better person? Here's a great role model for you to follow.

Search the headlines of every major newspaper in the world. Surf every Web site on the Internet. Watch CNN or FOX news twenty-four hours a day, seven days a week. You're *never* going to hear better news than these seven juicy tidbits you just read. And you're never going to have better news to share with others.

Plus, there's lots more good news where that came from. The Bible is full of promises, hope, encouragement, and assurance. But how will people know about all of this good news unless someone tells them? Consider the apostle Paul's words in Romans 10:11–15:

> As the Scriptures tell us, "Anyone who believes in him will not be disappointed." Jew and Gentile are the same in this respect. They all have the same Lord, who generously gives his riches to all who ask for them. For "Anyone who calls on the name of the Lord will be saved."
>
> But how can they call on him to save them unless they believe in him? And how can they believe in him if they have never heard about him? And how can they hear about him unless someone tells them? And how will anyone go and tell them without being sent? That is what the Scriptures mean when they say, "How beautiful are the feet of those who bring good news!"

Let's recap. If we don't have ears to hear the call to go and make disciples, we won't go. If we don't go, we won't be able to tell them. If no one tells them, they'll never hear about Him. If they never hear about Him, they'll never believe in Him. If they don't believe in Him, how will they ever be saved? Our motivation (or lack thereof) directly impacts the eternal lives of others who've not yet heard the good news.

Isn't spreading the good news of Christ's salvation the primary reason we aren't taken to heaven in a flash when we receive the Lord as our Savior? God leaves us here for a time so we can carry out His mission by delivering His good news to friends, family, and all those in our sphere of influence.

Let your beautiful feet deliver the good news of the gospel of Christ Jesus. Let your beautiful hands reach out to help others in Jesus' name. And let your beautiful lips be the means by which Christ can knock on the door of other people's hearts and minds.

HOLDING HIS HAND

Do I fear offending people with the good news of Jesus Christ? Why or why not?

_____

_____

_____

Are there things I need to do in order to get my feet moving in other people's direction so I can deliver this wonderful news I have discovered? If so, what might these things be?

_____

_____

_____

Holy Father,

We can't thank You enough for the extravagant love You've bestowed upon us and the positive impact this has on our past, present, and future. However, there are many who've failed to recognize just how "good" the good news of the gospel truly is. With Your help, we offer ourselves to be the feet, hands, and mouths that deliver Your good news to Your beloved people. In Jesus' name. Amen.

INFLUENCE A
GENERATION

Daily reading: Acts 11:19–30

Key passage: Then Barnabas went on to Tarsus to find Saul. When he found him, he brought him back to Antioch. Both of them stayed there with the church for a full year, teaching great numbers of people. (It was there at Antioch that the believers were first called Christians.) (Acts 11:25–26)

---

*L*ong before Bill Gates sparked a computer software revolution…before Sigmund Freud and Alfred Kinsey sparked sexual revolutions…even before George Washington and Abraham Lincoln sparked political revolutions…the apostle Paul, with the other disciples, sparked one of the greatest social, cultural, and spiritual revolutions the world has ever known (next to Jesus Himself, of course). In fact, our reading today tells us the teaching of Paul (Saul) and Barnabas led masses of people in Antioch to begin calling themselves *Christians*, a new term for followers of Christ that set them apart from other Gentiles and Jews.

Webster's online dictionary defines *revolution* as "a drastic and far-reaching change in ways of thinking and behaving." That's what Christ sought to bring about, and that's our mission as well. How did Paul spark such a change in the spiritual lives of so many people? How has he continued to impact countless lives? By creating ripple effects through his writing, traveling, and speaking efforts. This passionate penman wrote thirteen letters to various churches, most likely unaware that these letters would also serve as a template to guide all Christian churches throughout history. This prolific preacher traveled to untold numbers of cities and provinces throughout Asia Minor and Europe to tell people about his radical conversion experience. His motive wasn't to tell the world about himself, but rather to tell the world about the transformation God wants to bring about in people's lives, regardless of their ethnicity or of their worthiness.

What made Paul a prime candidate to become God's revolutionary? Many things combined. He had diligently studied Jewish law. He was incredibly familiar with the teachings of the prophets. He was learned in the Hebrew and Aramaic languages (Acts 21:40; 22:2–3; 23:6; Galatians 1:14; Philippians 3:5–6). He was familiar with Greek literature and culture, for his hometown of Tarsus was a hub of social and professional activity (Acts 21:37). Clearly, Paul was no dummy when it came to understanding the social, political, spiritual, and cultural climate of his society. He understood people and their traditions. He was comfortable in a variety of different environments. His high level of education meant that he could converse with intellectuals and other movers and shakers.

The Lord obviously recognized Paul's zeal for the Jewish traditions of his forefathers (Galatians 1:14), knowing that if his zeal was properly directed, Paul could be a tremendous asset to God's kingdom. Paul stopped at nothing to express his deep care and concern for the fledgling churches he established. He didn't allow imprisonment, painful torture, or even the threat of death to squelch his zeal for the gospel of Christ. If anything, these adverse circumstances most likely fueled Paul's revolutionary fire.

Even though Paul was a revolutionary, keep in mind that he didn't impact society to such a great degree overnight. In fact, do you realize how much time he spent in preparation for his writing and traveling ministry? Thirteen years! During this time, he reflected on Stephen's defense of the gospel. He prayed for a greater understanding of his personal conversion experience, and a deeper revelation of who Jesus really was. Paul considered how all of these things measured up against the Jewish law he had studied so passionately most of his life.[1] His deep understanding and personal revelations of these matters made him a prime candidate for the Holy Spirit to work through mightily in Antioch. There Paul greatly influenced not just a select few individuals, families, or churches, but much of the Roman Empire (Acts 13:1–3). His teaching reached "people throughout the province of Asia—both Jews and Greeks" (Acts 19:10).

What can we learn from the apostle Paul if we want to be revolutionaries for Christ? Primarily that no one becomes such a difference-maker overnight. However, there are things we can do every day that will make us better able to fulfill God's mission. We can diligently prepare for God to use us. We can pray earnestly. We must never stop learning more and more about who God is. We must seek to understand more and more about the Love Letter He has written to us. We must become students of the culture and times in which we live, recognizing why people do the things they do, and understanding why they should even be interested in hearing about a love relationship with Jesus Christ. Once we stop learning and engaging our culture, we lose touch with people and will forfeit many opportunities to attract others toward God's extravagant love.

At the ripe old age of eighteen, Alex and Brett Harris are engaging the culture and sparking a revolution among their generation. The two brothers became disturbed by the teenage trends of their generation, especially by our society's low expectations of teens and how young people seemed to be living up to them. So they decided to rebel—not against God or authority figures, but against the low expectations of an ungodly culture. Combining the words *rebellion* and *revolution*, these brothers are, in essence, rebelling against rebellion with their "Rebelution" concept (www.therebelution.com). Through their Web page, blogs, recommended reading lists, and conferences for parents and youth, their countercultural youth movement is rapidly spreading—not just across the country but across the world.

This movement encourages teens to reject the lies and corruption of the media-saturated youth culture, and to strive for the much higher levels of character and competence that the Bible urges us toward. Rather than chanting such worldly mantras as "Obey your thirst" and "Just do it," Alex and Brett introduced a new, explosive concept for teens—"Do Hard Things."

Their message is that by embracing challenges and hard work, teens can prepare for a brighter future and become an appreciated and respected segment of society, as they once were less than a century ago. By rebelling against the immaturity, irresponsibility, idleness, and indulgence that characterize their generation, young people can recognize their teen years as a "launching pad into a productive life of adulthood" rather than a "vacation from responsibility." Alex says, "Low expectations affect you even if you're not into the drugs, sex, etc., and it continues until someone intentionally remedies that irresponsibility."[2]

Of course, you don't have to be young to be an example or to impact a generation with a countercultural lifestyle. Young people need older, more spiritually mature people in their lives too. They need someone they can look up to and emulate; someone they can come to when they need a word of wisdom or encouragement; someone who is willing to offer insight based on their years of experience in walking with the Lord. Our children need grade-school teachers and college professors who believe in them and challenge them. They need Sunday-school teachers and youth pastors who will diligently impart biblical knowledge and counsel. They need examples of committed husbands and wives, godly fathers and mothers, and professional businessmen and women who display character and integrity.

Remember, today's youth will be tomorrow's husbands and wives, fathers and mothers, businesspeople, politicians, lawyers, doctors, and national leaders.

They'll be the ones weaving the moral and ethical fabric of the society you and I will grow old in. If we positively impact their generation today, they'll be better equipped to positively affect our generation and many generations to come.

HOLDING HIS HAND

When I think of the word *revolutionary*, who do I think of? Why?

_____

_____

_____

What might it look like if I took on the role of a cultural or spiritual revolutionary?

_____

_____

_____

How might I better prepare to be used by God to greatly impact my culture or generation for Christ?

_____

_____

_____

> *Lord Jesus,*
>
> *You were the ultimate revolutionary of all time, and we are privileged to have the opportunity, as Paul did, to follow in Your footsteps. Give us a passion to understand the world and the times in which we live. Show us how to appeal to all of those who are searching for true love and ultimate fulfillment, and help us point them squarely in Your direction. Amen.*

GIVE HOPE TO
THE HOPELESS

Daily reading: James 2:1–13

Key passage: Yes indeed, it is good when you truly obey our Lord's royal command found in the Scriptures: "Love your neighbor as yourself." But if you pay special attention to the rich, you are committing a sin, for you are guilty of breaking that law. (James 2:8–9)

---

*I*f you grew up poor in an underprivileged neighborhood with few opportunities for personal growth, what would you desire most? Chances are, you'd long for a one-way ticket out of poverty and hopelessness. People in desperate situations are more likely to get that one-way ticket when they have someone to believe in them and encourage them to pursue their dreams. Jerry Speight understands this, and he's chosen to do something about it.

When Jerry turned sixty-five in October 2005, some assumed that he'd be retiring soon, planning a life of leisure after his lengthy and successful sales career. Instead, he was planning the launch of a brand-new ministry in his hometown. Recognizing the overwhelming emotional, educational, financial, and spiritual needs of many underprivileged citizens of Greenville, Texas, as well as the abundant resources available to meet many of those needs, Jerry decided that the word *retirement* didn't need to be in his vocabulary just yet.

He formulated a vision for how the relatively successful in the community could rally around those in need and founded the Greenville Hope Center as a place where underprivileged youth and families could receive much-needed assistance. Through a variety of activities such as literacy and life-skills training, tutoring, and mentoring, the citizens of Greenville are helping to turn their inner-city neighbors' hopelessness and despair into determination to forge a better future for themselves and their families.

Of course, turning such a vision into a reality requires an enormous amount of resources and volunteer help. Gathering enough funds and friends to carry out this vision was a challenge that most would shy away from, but Jerry embraced it. First, he had to secure a facility. After searching every available building in the city, Jerry was elated when First Baptist Church offered their Family Life Center as the new home of the Greenville Hope Center, especially since this building was located in the heart of the inner-city community. Next, he had to recruit dozens of volunteers—public school teachers and juvenile probation officers who could help identify at-risk individuals in need of special training or job counseling, plus construction workers and technology experts who could help turn the facility into a state-of-the-art computer, math, and science training center.

In addition, Jerry had to raise thousands of dollars for renovations to the facility and to begin funding this enterprise. He applied for grants from individuals and corporate foundations, spoke to civic clubs and church groups, and scheduled meetings with some of the most financially influential members of the community. His vision spread rapidly. Within less than a year's time, the Greenville Hope Center went from a twinkle in Jerry Speight's eye to a tremendous asset in the community. Even high-school students who excel in certain subjects offer their time to tutor other students who've fallen behind. No one is too young or too old to help.

What difference has this asset made in Greenville, Texas? Perhaps you should ask Brenda and Fred. Brenda finished her high-school coursework, but failed her math exit examination. After failing the second time, she was referred to the Hope Center where she was connected with a family who was willing to spend a few hours per week tutoring her in math. Others also encouraged her, and after attempting the examination again, Brenda appeared in Jerry's office. "I passed my test! I'm getting my high-school diploma this afternoon!" she beamed.

Fred was a sixteen-year-old high-school dropout living with his three siblings at his grandmother's house because his mother had been in jail for the past fifteen years. Fred landed his first job at a Braum's Ice Cream and Dairy Store after participating in the Texas WorkForce program, which meets in the Hope Center. One day Fred stopped by on his two-mile walk home from work. Jerry offered to drive him the rest of the way and asked, "How do you get back and forth to work every day, Fred?"

"When my grandmother can't take me, I have to walk," Fred replied.

"Do you have a bicycle?" Jerry inquired.

Fred responded negatively.

One day Jerry was praising Fred's accomplishments to a local business owner, and in a matter of days the businessman presented Fred with a brand-new bicycle. He was so excited that he wouldn't get off long enough for the tires to be aired up. Now Fred is back in school and feeling more hopeful about his future than ever. Affirmation and acts of encouragement have given Fred a new perspective.

At one of the Hope Center's first fund-raising banquets, Jerry told the story of Fred receiving his new bike. Terdema Ussery, President and CEO of the Dallas Mavericks basketball team, also gave a touching speech about the power of hope in people's lives. Upon leaving the banquet, Mr. Ussery's sixteen-year-old son said, "Dad, I had no idea that something as small as a bicycle could impact someone's life so much!"

His father replied, "Son, where you live is not real life. Your peers often get BMWs for graduation, but that's not the real world. Fred lives in the real world—a world that we are called by God to impact with the blessings He gives us." Indeed, some people live in a world that others of us have never experienced—a world of poverty, addiction, crime, and hopelessness. Others have been extraordinarily blessed and can be an incredible blessing to those in need. Jerry is serving as a bridge to connect those two social groups.

The verse that keeps Jerry going with this ministry endeavor is Proverbs 13:12, "Hope deferred makes the heart sick, but a longing fulfilled is a tree of life" (NIV). Of course, Jerry's goal with the Greenville Hope Center is to lead people to the ultimate source of life, Jesus Christ.

Although he's reached retirement age, Jerry exclaims, "There's no time in a Christian's life that he can 'retire' from the responsibility we've been given to serve Christ by serving others. There's simply not a place in Scripture that we can point to and say, 'I'm relieved of my duties. I'll let a younger person step in and take over from here.'" Realizing his days are numbered (as are all of our days), Jerry wisely continues to offer hope to the hopeless, all in the name of Jesus Christ.

If Jerry Speight's name rings a bell, it's because I've mentioned him a couple of times in this series. He's the man I wrote about in *Completely His;* he told Gary Jarstfer of his wife's death and he called me the day of the accident. He's also the one who first looked at my Women at the Well lecture notes and encouraged me to turn them into a book. And he is a man I deeply admire, a man who comfortably rubs elbows with powerful and poor people alike, offering hope and inspiration with his completely irresistible life.

HOLDING HIS HAND

Do I gravitate toward people who are "like me" or in the same tier of the social ladder? Why or why not?

_____

_____

_____

Do I know people who are less privileged in life who need to hear the gospel of Jesus Christ? Do I know folks who are far more privileged than I am who also need to hear of God's love? If so, who are these people, and how might I approach them?

_____

_____

_____

What would it look like for me to show favor to everyone, regardless of their social status? Is this something I am motivated to do? Why or why not?

_____

_____

_____

Heavenly Father,

_Thank You for the many blessings You bestow upon us. We
acknowledge there are many people in this world, some
who have less, some who have more, who need to hear of
Your saving grace. Give us favor with men and women
from all walks of life, so that we can effectively draw them
toward Your extravagant love. Amen._

OPEN YOUR HEART
AND HOME

Daily reading: Acts 16:11–15, 40; Philippians 1:1–11

Key passage: On the Sabbath we went a little way outside the city to a riverbank, where we supposed that some people met for prayer, and we sat down to speak with some women who had come together. One of them was Lydia from Thyatira, a merchant of expensive purple cloth. She was a worshiper of God. As she listened to us, the Lord opened her heart, and she accepted what Paul was saying. She was baptized along with other members of her household, and she asked us to be her guests. "If you agree that I am faithful to the Lord," she said, "come and stay at my home." And she urged us until we did. (Acts 16:13–15)

*M*any people compare themselves to great evangelists, speakers, writers, or Bible teachers and conclude, "God could never use me like that." If that's been your feeling, prepare yourself for a paradigm shift. What if I told you that drawing others toward God's extravagant love can be as easy as opening your front door to people? That's what Lydia did, and God brought about a harvest of great things as a result. Let me tell you the story.

In Jesus' day Jewish law stated that a synagogue could only be formed by the coming together of at least ten male heads of households, but when such a group didn't exist in a town, people would come together for worship under an open sky or near a body of water.[1] Because Lydia and her friends had no synagogue in Philippi, they often gathered to worship and pray along the riverbank. One day Paul and Silas saw the group and sat down to speak with them. In these simple surroundings, Paul told Lydia the gospel and then baptized her in the river along with her entire household. Afterward she insisted on hosting the apostles in her own home, allowing them time to become deeply rooted in her community. Lydia's hospitality was the "seed" that caused a mighty church to soon rise up in Philippi. Paul's reference to the elders and deacons in the opening of his letter to the Philippian church indicates that the believers grew significantly in number as well as in spiritual maturity.

Through Lydia's hospitality, Paul drew many Philippians toward God's extravagant love. Had Lydia not opened her heart and home to these apostles, Paul's evangelistic efforts may not have taken root. We should never underestimate the power of warm and loving hospitality.

My friend Bonnie, whom I affectionately refer to as the Martha Stewart of Tyler, Texas, reminds me of Lydia. While lots of women can cook and keep house, I've never seen a woman do it with such love and enthusiasm for her family, friends, and church members as Bonnie does. She comes alive by creating masterpieces such as homemade sourdough bread from a seventeen-year-old starter (it gets better with age) or an elaborate sugar-cookie nativity scene complete with all of the characters and animals (I got to eat baby Jesus!). Bonnie's charming home is beautifully decorated, and when I'm her guest I just want to settle into a comfy chair by the fireplace and enjoy the warm ambience, hot tea, friendly conversation, and delectable food. The young moms Bonnie's mentored have also been the beneficiaries of her knack for entertaining as they've been treated to wonderful outdoor dinners by the lake. Bonnie gives people a taste (pun intended) of God's great love for them by creating special moments like these.

Bonnie has four children, all of whom have enjoyed many years of having their friends over to hang out (and pig out, I'm sure!). Even when you can't come to her home, Bonnie will send care packages of God's love in your direction. When some of her children left for college, Bonnie sent them homemade goodies to share with their friends. What is Bonnie's spiritual gift? Hospitality! But it's not just God's gift to *her*—it's God's gift to *all* who know her!

If hospitality is your spiritual gift, girlfriend, don't hide it under a bushel. Offer it to God and to others with confidence that it truly does make a difference. Host a Bible study in your home, or offer to throw a bridal or baby shower for a newcomer to your church, or invite visiting missionaries to stay in your home. As Hebrews 13:2 says, "Don't forget to show hospitality to strangers, for some who have done this have entertained angels without realizing it!"

HOLDING HIS HAND

Can I open my home to people? What are some things I thoroughly enjoy doing for other people? Do I see these things as an evangelistic tool? Why or why not?

_____

_____

_____

Do I refrain from inviting guests over because I'm too overwhelmed by the idea of getting everything perfect for company? What might be the root of such perfectionistic standards?

_____

_____

_____

If we let go of our pride and fear of what other people will think of our house, our furniture, our cooking, or our children's manners, might there be more that God could do through us to help spread the gospel of Christ to those who come into our homes?

Dear God,

We long to open not just our hearts to You, but our homes also. You've given them to us, and we want to give them back to You to use in accomplishing Your agenda and fulfilling Your purposes. Give us the confidence to invite others into our homes and the ability to comfort and encourage them in their walk with You. In Jesus' name. Amen.

BECOME A CONFIDENT WOMAN

Daily reading: 1 Corinthians 14:34–35; Titus 2:1–5

Key passage: Similarly, teach the older women to live in a way that is appropriate for someone serving the Lord. They must not go around speaking evil of others and must not be heavy drinkers. Instead, they should teach others what is good. These older women must train the younger women to love their husbands and their children, to live wisely and be pure, to take care of their homes, to do good, and to be submissive to their husbands. Then they will not bring shame on the word of God. (Titus 2:3–5)

---

*W*hen I began teaching at Teen Mania Ministries in 1999, I anticipated leading young people into a deeper relationship with Christ. The first class I taught was an *Experiencing God* Bible study for anyone who wanted to come. I got so pumped as I witnessed both male and female college-age students develop a greater understanding of God's purpose for their lives.

But one day I almost allowed a young man to burst my bubble. He approached me at the copy machine and said, "I hear several interns speak highly of your Bible study, Mrs. Ethridge." I thanked him for his kind words, but I wasn't prepared for what came next.

"But how do you justify teaching the Bible when you are a woman?"

I was flabbergasted. *What kind of church had this kid grown up in that women weren't allowed to teach the Bible?* While women have come a long way in gaining respect as effective evangelists, be aware that as a woman you may come up against some resistance as you try to serve God. I believe this resistance comes from a misunderstanding of Paul's teaching.

At first glance, Paul may appear to be saying two different things about a woman's role. In 1 Corinthians 14, he says that women are to be "silent" in the church. However, in Titus he instructs women to teach and train other women. So which is it? Are women to be silent, or are we to teach and train? As we discussed in *Completely His*, we must perform a historical, cultural, and contextual analysis to truly exegete (properly understand and personally apply) a passage of Scripture.

In the 1 Corinthians passage, Paul is addressing the issue of orderly worship. During the time of his writings, women were not educated, and it was a cultural norm for them to sit on one side of the church while men sat on the other side. If the speaker was explaining something that the women failed to understand, many would yell across the aisle to ask their husbands for an explanation, even as the speaker was trying to speak. Imagine the chaos this would create in a church service! So to restore order in worship services, Paul instructed these uneducated, outspoken, and sometimes rude women to

be silent [or nondisruptive] during the church meetings. It is not proper for them to speak [when the speaker is talking]. They should be submissive [or respectful], just as the law says. If they have any questions to ask, let them ask their [educated] husbands at home, for it is improper for women to speak in [or disrupt] church meetings. (1 Corinthians 14:34–35)

In light of the context of this passage, I believe that Paul was correcting women who were being rude, *not* restricting their right to pray, prophesy, or spread the gospel.

Unfortunately, many throughout church history have misunderstood this passage to mean that women should have no voice at all in the church. When you have no voice inside the church, it's easy to lose confidence in your voice outside of the church as well. Effective evangelism becomes impossible when we question our role in the body of Christ.

Examining the Titus passage, some might say that women are allowed to teach and train other women, but not men. Again, let us understand the times in which this passage was written. Culturally, it would not have made sense to allow women to teach because they were uneducated, and men were taught separate from the women. However, today's culture is very different. Many women are highly educated, and Bible classes are often coed. This fact, coupled with Acts 18:26, which tells us that Apollos received teaching from Priscilla, leads me to believe that God does not have an issue with women teaching men, especially if the men submit willingly to that teaching.

Considering that two-thirds of Christians are female, this poses an interesting question. If the devil can distort God's Word and cause two-thirds of believers to feel God has placed a muzzle over their mouths when they are in His house, he has succeeded in incapacitating a large number of potential evangelists. We can't let Satan falsely use God's words to strip us of our passion to minister to believers and to draw others toward God's love.

Women are indeed called to teach and disciple others, especially other women. While we don't need "feminazis," who try to obnoxiously rule and reign *over* men, we do need women who are confident enough to come *alongside* men and do that which only women can do. What male pastor can step out of his pulpit and intimately connect with the heart of a woman in order to disciple her over a long period of time? He would run the risk of getting too emotionally involved with her, or at the very least, give others the impression of an inappropriate relationship. That's simply not wise. We need *women* to step up to the plate and minister to other women—to learn God's Word, then effectively teach, train, counsel, and encourage other women. We need to express concern for the spiritual growth of our sisters, cry with them, laugh with them, and form relationships in which women can truly heal and learn to trust again. This is the best way for a woman to experience God's healing touch and to deepen her trust in Him—by being in a relationship with another woman who resembles Jesus.

As a female follower of Jesus Christ, do not allow biblical ignorance or antiquated cultural standards to restrict your freedom to minister to others with the gospel of Jesus Christ. Just as Jesus called and worked through Mary Magdalene, Martha, Joanna, Lydia, Priscilla, Susanna, and a multitude of other women, He can use you for His great glory as well.

HOLDING HIS HAND

Have I hesitated to disciple others because I feel it isn't a woman's place to teach the gospel? If so, why?

_____

_____

_____

Does understanding the true meaning of Paul's words when he instructed that women should remain "silent" in the church give me more confidence to pray, prophesy, and teach? Why or why not?

_____

_____

_____

If all women understood their calling as the bride of Christ and confidently shared His love with others, what would the results be for God's kingdom? for individual lives?

_____

_____

_____

Almighty Creator,

Thank You that Your plan for the salvation of the world includes women—not just that we be saved, but that we become instrumental in saving others. Give us a renewed sense of passion for reaching out into the world with Christ's love, and show us how to encourage other women to do the same. In Jesus' most holy and precious name. Amen.

BE AN ENCOURAGER

Daily reading: Acts 4:32–37; 11:22–24

Key passage: When [Barnabas] arrived and saw this proof of God's favor, he was filled with joy, and he encouraged the believers to stay true to the Lord. Barnabas was a good man, full of the Holy Spirit and strong in faith. And large numbers of people were brought to the Lord. (Acts 11:23–24)

*D*o loved ones ever refer to you by a nickname instead of your real name? Most nicknames are terms of endearment. When we were growing up, my parents affectionately referred to my brother, Bill, and sister, Donna, as Bubba and Sissy. (My nickname was Little Booger, but that's a different story.) I call my daughter Erin-Doodle because when she was a baby, she'd turn over on her side and curl up like a doodlebug when we laid her in the crib. I call my son Matt-Man because he loves superheroes or Mister Mattster Monster when he's behaving more like a beast than a boy.

You've probably heard or read the name Barnabas plenty of times, but did you realize that Barnabas wasn't his real name? According to Acts 4:36, his given name was Joseph.

The name Barnabas means "son of encouragement," and Barnabas seems to have lived up to his name, which is perhaps an explanation of where it came from. Verse 37 tells us he gave generously to those in need, selling personal property and donating all of the money to the apostles so they could distribute it to the poor. Barnabas was reputed to be "a good man, full of the Holy Spirit and strong in faith" (Acts 11:24).

When concerns arose over the church in Antioch, Barnabas's Jewish colleagues sent him to check things out. He sensed that God's favor was on these new Gentile converts, and he was thrilled they had become believers in Christ. He wasn't concerned that they weren't Jewish, and he encouraged them to "stay true to the Lord" (Acts 11:23). In fact, everywhere he went, Barnabas encouraged people in their faith. He brought many to the Lord during his missionary journeys with Paul and John Mark.

Marcy Graves is a "Barnabas" in her own right. As director of cardiopulmonary neurodiagnostics at Harris Methodist Southwest Hospital, she came up with a fun idea for encouraging patients. Inspired by the movie *Patch Adams*, she started a clown troupe that calls itself the "Ha HaS" (Healing and Humor at Southwest). Every Wednesday afternoon this team of medical professionals transform themselves into gleeful clowns. They go from the fourth floor all the way down to the emergency room, spreading laughter and encouragement from room to room to patients of all ages. My friend Susan Duke tells their story in her inspiring book, *Earth Angels*, explaining:

> Marcy magically becomes Nurse Ducky, donning an old-fashioned nurse's uniform, a bulging red nose, an oversized nurse's hat, and three-inch-long eyelashes embellished with rhinestones. Her sidekick, a duck puppet named Quackers, dresses just like Nurse Ducky and flirts with all the male patients.
>
> Other characters include Dr. Cat Scan, who dresses as a cat and carries a huge magnifying glass; Photo Kitty, who takes pictures of patients (actually exaggerated cartoon caricatures that

Marcy draws); and Smiley Bubbles, who blows bubbles into every room and seems to make older patients especially happy! The troupe also includes Dr. Feel-Good; the Health and Healing Fairy; and Dee, a former patient who wears heart-shaped eyeglasses and juggles very badly. (When Dee was seriously ill, she declared that if she recovered she would join this team of joyful earth angels whose laughter had helped her so much!)[1]

One day Marcy received an unexpected call at the hospital. It was the real Dr. Patch Adams from the Gesundheit! Institute in West Virginia. He'd heard about Marcy's clown troupe and invited her to go to China on an "Ambassadors of Love and Caring" tour. Doctors, nurses, respiratory therapists, and even a few professional clowns met in Los Angeles, then flew to Hong Kong, Shanghai, Beijing, and Nanjing, visiting hospitals, orphanages, and hospices. Although the Chinese patients didn't understand English, they understood that this team had come to make them smile. Like Christ's love, humor and encouragement transcend language and cultural barriers.

Of course, encouragement isn't limited to giving to the poor or visiting the sick. We only have to use our imagination to think of ways to bring a smile to someone's face or heart. For example, when my friend Katie flew to Michigan to speak before thousands of people, I created tiny slips of paper with various scriptures, rolled them up, stuffed them into empty capsule containers (available at local drugstores), and placed them in a prescription bottle with a label saying, "TAKE 1 TO 2 CAPSULES AS NEEDED FOR ENCOURAGEMENT."

A big hug, a pat on the back, a kind word or phone call—even a friendly smile—can brighten someone's day. You may not think that's enough to lead others to Christ, but your simple, loving gestures may bring these people back to you for answers when they are struggling or searching for meaning in life. They are not going to run to the solemn or straight-faced for encouragement. They are going to run to an irresistible someone—someone like you.

HOLDING HIS HAND

Can I remember a time in my life when I needed encouragement and someone came through for me? What did he or she do? How did it impact me?

_____

_____

_____

If I was interested in having a conversation about spiritual matters, who
would I gravitate toward? What is it about that person that encourages me to
go in their direction? How can I emulate those qualities?

_____

_____

_____

Even if I only sow spiritual seeds in someone's life but never get to harvest
them, do I think encouraging others is worth the effort? Do I find myself
encouraged when I encourage others? Why or why not?

_____

_____

_____

> *Dear Heavenly Father,*
>
> *Help us take our eyes off our own problems long enough to*
> *recognize those in this world who need encouragement.*
> *Whether it is a smile, a hug, a kind word, or a measure of*
> *financial assistance, let us offer whatever You lead us to*
> *give with a happy heart. Amen.*

WALK THE WALK

Daily reading: James 1–5

Key passage: Dear brothers and sisters, what's the use of saying you have faith if you don't prove it by your actions? That kind of faith can't save anyone. (James 2:14)

---

*T*alk is cheap.

Put your money where your mouth is.

Actions speak louder than words.

You can talk the talk, but can you walk the walk?

Although these are contemporary sayings, James obviously shared these sentiments. Throughout his writings, he exhorts believers to be genuine Christians, not just with their lips but also with their lives. He challenges us to be not just readers or speakers of God's Word, but also doers of the Word (James 1:22–25). We can't just talk about helping people *in theory*. We have to reach out and help them *in actuality*.

I recently met a woman, Myra Noyes, whom I believe embodies this concept. Myra has gone to great lengths to minister to people who have often been shunned—shunned by churches full of folks who talked a good Christian talk but refused to walk the Christian walk alongside those who needed a helping hand.

In 1990, Myra started attending a support group for gays and lesbians wanting to leave the homosexual lifestyle. A singles minister, she wanted to learn more about what people who struggle with same-sex attraction needed in order to overcome their struggle. She found no resources in her hometown of Jacksonville, Florida, but then she heard about a support group on a Focus on the Family radio interview with the president of Exodus International (an organization that ministers to and equips homosexuals to come out of "the lifestyle").

During one of those meetings, God rocked her world with a major revelation of just how badly this group of lesbian women were hurting. The discussion leader wrote the heading "Friends" on the whiteboard, then began making a list of people or things, asking the question, "Is this a friend? If so, I'll leave it written on the board. If not, I'll erase it." The leader began with the words *drugs* and *alcohol*, which the group unanimously decided were not friends. Next she wrote *father*, and after some discussion, the group agreed that this word could remain on the board. Then she wrote *mother*, and every woman in the room insisted that *mother* was not a friend, so the word was erased. (A homosexual often struggles with a dysfunctional relationship with the same-sex parent.)

Then, the leader wrote *p-a-s...* and before she could finish, the group exploded with fierce anger. "No! Do NOT write that word!" Myra was stunned by the venomous outbursts and shocked to hear story after story of how these women had been so deeply wounded by their *pastors*. One woman told of how gossip about her past got around to her music minister. When he confronted her, she hid nothing. She replied, "Yes, it's true that I used to be a lesbian, but that's not where I am anymore. I've been celibate and faithful to God for almost four years." Even so, he kicked her out of the choir with the support of the pastor of the church.

Another woman told about how she had broken free from a lesbian affair when she was sixteen, but when the news later reached her youth pastor, he banned her from youth group, Sunday school, and from working in the nursery. She was only allowed to attend worship, but was not allowed to be around any kids in the church, as he assumed she must be a sexual predator.

All of these women had either left their churches or been kicked out of their churches. Myra was horrified that the very institution and individuals that should be embracing and ministering to these hurting people were adding insult to injury. They had been made to feel judged, rejected, condemned, and hopeless.

On the way home, Myra's heart ached for these women she had grown to love so much. Through tears, she cried out to God, *Lord, who can help these women overcome their fear and hatred of the church?* At that moment, she heard God whisper in her heart, *It's you, Myra. You are the one I want.*

Myra had every reason to argue with God. She already had a full-time job as a singles minister. Not only that, but she and her husband, Don, had two biological children, nine adopted children, and several grandchildren. Their plate was full. But the burden was undeniable, and the calling from God crystal clear.

Myra and Don invited people from their church over for a cookout and prayer meeting for discernment on how to start a ministry to the homosexual community in the Jacksonville area. They knew they'd have to host the meetings in a more neutral location than in the church, if people were going to feel free to come. They'd have to rent a place, but that would cost money. They took up an offering that night and collected over two thousand dollars, which would soon be multiplied into several thousand more—enough to rent a storefront location for the first eight years.

Eventually, various churches caught the vision and started similar groups on their own. Myra continues to host meetings at Deermeadows Baptist Church for parents and families of those struggling with same-sex attraction.

In her seventeenth year of ministry to the homosexual community, she's ministered to thousands of individuals and families who simply didn't know where else to turn.

Myra's love and faith in God's redemptive purposes is completely irresistible, and God is using her in wonderful ways. She has offered herself as an agent of reconciliation between God and His people, regardless of their past deeds or the emotional baggage they carry. She simply loves them as God does—right where they are, just as they are.

Is God inviting you to walk more deeply with Him by walking more closely alongside others? Are there people He's asking you to demonstrate His love toward that will require more understanding, effort, and compassion than what you currently possess? Don't worry. As Myra will testify, He'll give you everything you need if you are ready to draw others toward His extravagant love through *your* irresistible Christian walk.

HOLDING HIS HAND

Have I ever been around a Christian who talks a good talk but fails to walk a good walk? How did it make me feel about that person? about God?

_____

_____

_____

_____

Is there anything in my life that would cause someone else to feel the same way about me? Is there an area of my life where I talk a good talk but fail to walk a good walk?

_____

_____

_____

_____

If I were to sell myself out to become a full-fledged doer of God's word, how might that impact another's life? How would it impact my life?

_____

_____

_____

_____

Father God,

We acknowledge that sometimes we spout high and lofty words with our lips, but we fail to live up to those standards with our lives. Help us to not just talk the talk, but also walk the walk so that others will see that You have truly transformed us. Use us to convince others that their lives can be transformed as well. Amen.

Model Integrity

Daily reading: Titus 2:7–8; Jude 1

Key passage: And you yourself must be an example to them by doing good deeds of every kind. Let everything you do reflect the integrity and seriousness of your teaching. Let your teaching be so correct that it can't be criticized. Then those who want to argue will be ashamed because they won't have anything bad to say about us. (Titus 2:7–8)

*I*n recent months, there've been multiple exposés about good people doing bad things. CEOs of major corporations have been caught with their hands in the company ledgers, embezzling funds from their employees and shareholders, and erasing any paper trails that might incriminate them. Military recruiters have been caught lying on videotape, minimizing the potential threats of joining the service so they can meet their monthly quotas of young recruits. Hurricane victims have been discovered submitting fraudulent claims to insurance companies to reap benefits to which they are not entitled. Even an evangelical pastor who preached God's Word from Sunday to Sunday was accused of doing drugs and having a sexual relationship outside of marriage on other days of the week. Christians often wonder, *Is there* *anyone worthy of respect? Anyone who can be trusted? Anyone who acts with integrity?*

It's sad but true that the media's attention isn't grabbed as easily by those who *do* act with integrity as it is by those who *don't*. Lots of airtime is dedicated to those folks who fall from grace, but as Jude, the half brother of Jesus encouraged, we need to be careful that we "aren't contaminated by their sins" (verse 23).

In Jude's opening lines, he confesses that his original intent was to deliver a message about Christ's salvation. However, he suddenly felt as if he had to write about a different topic altogether—defending the truth of the gospel message—because "some godless people have wormed their way in among you, saying that God's forgiveness allows us to live immoral lives" (verse 4).

Jude wants us to know that just because others had killed their consciences enough to commit a certain sin, it doesn't mean we should become desensitized to sin. He urges us to go in the opposite direction, continually thinking of ways to encourage and spur one another (and ourselves) toward "outbursts of love and good deeds" (Hebrews 10:24). Rather than waste our energies throwing stones at those who lack integrity, let us invest our energies in modeling integrity, as well as praising others who do the same.

Greg and I have spent the past few years singing the praises of a man of integrity we had the pleasure of working with. As we began the building and remodeling process to double the size of our modest log cabin home, we expected that we'd have problems with the builder. We'd heard horror stories about how people often felt cheated out of tons of money and were dissatisfied with the quality of the finished product when they embarked on massive construction projects with even the most reputable of builders. We interviewed three potential contractors, and we hired Craig Klaassen, mainly because he was the only one I felt I could yell at if necessary.

But because of Craig's integrity, we never had any reason to yell or even worry. He'd find things we would never have noticed in a million years and demand they be redone correctly (even at his own expense if necessary). We grew to trust him completely, and he lifted our spirits each day that he strolled through the house whistling his favorite hymns. With all of the time, money, and energy we poured into the project, it stood a fair chance of becoming our worst nightmare, but Craig and his crew were an absolute dream to work with.

Would people say the same of you? Would they say that interacting with you gives them hope that not everyone's moral compass has turned south in our society? Would they have their faith restored that there are still people on the planet who provide a clear glimpse into God's character? Do you model integrity to all those who know you? In doing so, you will set a stellar example for others to follow of how a bride of Christ looks, walks, talks, thinks, acts, and interacts with others.

HOLDING HIS HAND

If I had a fly on the wall of my office listening to every word I speak with clients, employees, supervisors, and friends, would I consistently set a strong example of integrity? Why or why not?

_____

_____

_____

_____

What if the fly moved onto the walls of my home? Do I model integrity with my husband and children? Why or why not?

_____

_____

_____

_____

What, if anything, needs to change in order for me to model integrity?

_____

_____

_____

_____

Lord Jesus,

*You came to earth to set the ultimate example of integrity.
Help us to follow that example every day with the thoughts
we entertain, the words we speak, the actions we engage in,
the places we go, and the people we encounter. May others
see You more clearly because of what they see in us. Amen.*

Live Loved

Daily reading: John 13:23; 19:26; 20:2; 21:7, 20; Ephesians 3:14–21

Key passage: And may you have the power to understand, as all God's people should, how wide, how long, how high, and how deep his love really is. May you experience the love of Christ, though it is so great you will never fully understand it. Then you will be filled with the fullness of life and power that comes from God. (Ephesians 3:18–19)

I love you…from the bottom of the deepest ocean, to the top of the moon, around the sun, through all the stars in every galaxy, and all the way down to the bottom of the ocean again…times a bazillion infinities!" When my children were younger and less burdened with the stuff of teen life, this was our simple way of saying good night to each other. As I tucked them in, gently kissed the tip of their noses, and prayed that God would give them sweet rest, I could hear the wheels in their minds turning. As soon as there was a break in the conversation, they would be the first to initiate the nightly the routine. "I love you, Mommy, from the bottom of the deepest ocean…"

One day Matthew asked, "Mom, how far is it to the bottom of the deepest ocean? And to the top of the moon? And all around the sun and the stars in every galaxy?" Of course, I had no idea, nor was I particularly inspired to consult the science journals or the Internet to find the answer to my son's questions. I knew what he was really asking—"*How much* do you love me?"

Isn't that our question as well—not of our earthly parent, perhaps, but of our heavenly Parent? Don't we want to know how much God loves us? I suspect Paul knew this, and that's why he wrote the church at Ephesus that he wanted them to know "how wide, how long, how high, and how deep" God's love really is (Ephesians 3:18).

Of course, no human who has walked this planet could possibly understand such an incomprehensible love as what God has for His children. However, John seems to have come close. As atypical as today's reading is (looking at individual verses in John's gospel rather than an entire passage of Scripture), I hope you get the point. Over and over, John describes himself in a unique way, displaying incredible confidence in his intimate relationship with Jesus.

John continually identified himself as "the disciple whom Jesus loved":
- While sitting in the upper room.
- While standing at the foot of the cross holding Mary in his arms.
- As he received shocking reports that Jesus' body was no longer in the tomb.
- While he was fishing in the sea in the wee hours of the morning.
- While he was following Jesus and Peter as they conversed with one another.

Obviously, knowledge of God's love for him flooded every inch of John's heart. It rested securely in his bones, joints, and marrow. It was deeply embedded in every nerve and fiber of his body until it became his identity. Any disciple who consistently refers to himself as the *one* whom Jesus loved was obviously very secure in that relationship. John lived loved. In his mind, it didn't matter who else Jesus loved. Their relationship was special, intimate, and exclusive.

The church I grew up in had a special group of women who exuded this same security and confidence. My mom's Little Flock Sunday-school class has met together now for over forty years, celebrating Christ's infinite love for us, and their love for one another. I was so blessed to grow up in the midst of such women. We lived in a small town, so most of these women knew my every shameful act and dirty deed as a teenage girl. Yet every week they showered me with hugs and verbal reminders that "Jesus loves you! And we love you too!"

I think we can all learn a lesson from John and the Little Flock ladies. What would our lives be like if a full knowledge of God's unconditional love was firmly planted in our brains and filled every square inch of our hearts? What if we, too, lived loved? What if we felt God's love so deeply that we could even sense it in our bones, joints, and marrow, and in every fiber and nerve of our bodies? Would it radically transform the way we think, ridding our minds of some of the "stinking thinking" that we do about ourselves? Would it impact our moods and emotions to know without a doubt we are truly and deeply loved, in spite of our shortcomings? Would it improve our outlook on life, our relationships, and our energy levels? Would such knowledge inspire us to have a greater confidence in talking with others about the love affair we share with our heavenly Bridegroom? You bet it would.

Despite how you may feel about yourself, you are loved. Not just liked. Not just tolerated. But loved. The God of the universe loves you—passionately, deeply, tenderly, unconditionally. Once you've got that fact firmly rooted and established in your life, it's going to bear fruit. Others are going to notice something incredibly special about you. They are going to want some of whatever you've got. When they ask, tell them, "I've got a heavenly Bridegroom who sweeps me off my feet every day with His lavish love for me!" But don't stop there. Toss the bouquet in their direction. Tell them that God loves them just as passionately and is pursuing them just as fervently. Tell them that they, too, can live loved.

HOLDING HIS HAND

What do I think God feels about me, and why?

_____

_____

_____

How would it affect me if I knew in my bones that God loves me completely and unconditionally?

_____

_____

_____

How might I influence others to recognize God's lavish love for them if they were able to see this passionate relationship demonstrated so clearly in me?

_____

_____

_____

> _Loving Lord,_
>
> _How we crave the confidence that John demonstrated as he continually referred to himself as the one whom You loved. Give us a fuller knowledge of the fact that You love us so completely, passionately, and unconditionally, and help us inspire others to recognize the same about themselves. In Jesus' name. Amen._

See Both Sides

Daily reading: Revelation 1; 19:1–10; 21:1–14

Key passage: And the one sitting on the throne said, "Look, I am making all things new!" And then he said to me, "Write this down, for what I tell you is trustworthy and true." And he also said, "It is finished! I am the Alpha and the Omega—the Beginning and the End. To all who are thirsty I will give the springs of the water of life without charge! All who are victorious will inherit all these blessings, and I will be their God, and they will be my children." (Revelation 21:5–7)

---

*M*y first trip to the principal's office occurred the year I was in kindergarten. What was my crime? Kissing Tom Davidson on the cheek during milk break. I don't remember what prompted me to do such a thing, but I remember the terror in the pit of my stomach as a teacher marched me out of the cafeteria and into Mr. Donovan's office.

His secretary told me to plant myself on a blue leather chair and wait for Mr. Donovan to arrive. With wide eyes, I stared around his office walls—dark-stained oak paneling adorned by numerous shiny awards and photographs. To me, his mahogany desk seemed almost as big as a school bus, and although I wasn't clear about its meaning, the "Discipline Creates Disciples" plaque on his desktop gave me the impression that I was in big trouble.

Sure enough, I got a light paddling that day, which hurt my ego worse than my rump. I left Mr. Donovan's office confused as to what was so terrible about kissing someone on the cheek—my parents did it to me every day. Whenever I overheard a teacher asking a student, "Do you want to go to the principal's office?" terror overwhelmed me once again. My trip to the principal's office helped me keep my nose clean, which was a good thing—I didn't get sent to the principal's office again until the sixth grade. But how sad that this early encounter with Mr. Donovan prevented me from recognizing his wonderfully warm, friendly, and loving side until years later. My view of him was one sided.

I suspect many of us make the same mistake in our view of God. We see Him as just, but not compassionate, holy but not loving. We see Him as a distant disciplinarian ready to punish us big time if we step too far out of line. We try to be good, but often sense we are failing. We avoid Him at all costs, because we fear big trouble if we wind up "in His office." When we go to Him in prayer, we envision the spiritual spankings we deserve from His hand.

While it's true that God gently disciplines us, it's not because He is angry with us or because He is meanspirited or vindictive. God disciplines us because He loves us and wants us to become better people and better disciples.

John understood *both* sides of Jesus—His wonderfully warm, friendly, and loving side as well as His disciplinarian side. In the book of Revelation, John emphasizes God's desire for holiness, writing letters of warning to the seven churches and penning such words as...

- His judgments are just and true. He has punished the great prostitute who corrupted the earth with her immorality, and he has avenged the murder of his servants. (Revelation 19:2)
- But cowards who turn away from me, and unbelievers, and the corrupt, and murderers, and the immoral, and those who practice witchcraft, and idol worshipers, and all liars—their doom is in the

lake that burns with fire and sulfur. This is the second death.
(Revelation 21:8)

John also envisions Jesus as a lovesick Bridegroom who's on a mission to rescue, redeem, and betroth Himself to His beautiful bride...

- Then I heard again what sounded like the shout of a huge crowd, or the roar of mighty ocean waves, or the crash of loud thunder: "Hallelujah! For the Lord our God, the Almighty, reigns. Let us be glad and rejoice and honor him. For the time has come for the wedding feast of the Lamb, and his bride has prepared herself. She is permitted to wear the finest white linen." (Fine linen represents the good deeds done by the people of God.)

  And the angel said, "Write this: Blessed are those who are invited to the wedding feast of the Lamb." And he added, "These are true words that come from God." (Revelation 19:6–9)

- And I saw the holy city, the new Jerusalem, coming down from God out of heaven like a beautiful bride prepared for her husband. (Revelation 21:2)

- Then one of the seven angels who held the seven bowls containing the seven last plagues came and said to me, "Come with me! I will show you the bride, the wife of the Lamb." (Revelation 21:9)

Most likely, John was entrusted with these visions and prophecies about the future return of Jesus Christ because he understood both the holiness of God and the love of God.

As we draw others toward God's extravagant love, we also need to present a balanced view of God. If we focus entirely on the disciplinarian side, people will see God as a perfectionist who never enjoys His imperfect people. Their relationship with Him will become a source of frustration and guilt as they stumble and fall, as all human beings do. Yet if we focus entirely on the merciful side, people may get the impression that striving for personal holiness isn't a necessary component of the Christian life.

Yes, God wants people to clean up their act, but He recognizes that we can't do that without His love on our side. It takes more than fear and intimidation to inspire lasting change. It takes the understanding that God's love for us is unconditional and He's never going to give up on us. This incredible love inspires us to live a holy life as a way of expressing our gratitude for God's unending grace, mercy, and love.

As we help others recognize and embrace both sides of our just and compassionate God, they will be inspired to pursue both holiness and intimacy with their loving heavenly Bridegroom.

HOLDING HIS HAND

How do I view God? What do I think is important to Him, and why?

_____

_____

_____

When I talk to people about God, what do I usually emphasize? His disciplinarian side or His warm, loving side? How do they usually respond?

_____

_____

_____

Most Holy God,

Thank You for providing such wonderful incentive to pursue personal holiness. Inspire us to show our reciprocal love for You by submitting to Your loving discipline, and help us encourage others to do the same. Amen.

BE A SPIRITUAL HERO

Daily reading: Philippians 2:25–30

Key passage: Welcome [Epaphroditus] with Christian love and with great joy, and be sure to honor people like him. For he risked his life for the work of Christ, and he was at the point of death while trying to do for me the things you couldn't do because you were far away. (Philippians 2:29–30)

---

*F*irefighters who reenter burning buildings to save one more life… soldiers who throw themselves on top of grenades to spare the lives of their military buddies…police officers who engage in high-speed chases and step into the line of fire in order to serve and protect the public. Everybody loves and appreciates a hero.

Of course, some heroes go unrecognized: hospice nurses who keep dying patients comfortable and share the families' sorrow…teachers who invest extra hours tutoring a student who has far more potential than her report card reflects…mothers who give up nice paychecks and little luxuries so they can afford to stay at home with their babies. While a few heroes have their praises sung on television talk shows or in local newspaper articles, our world is filled with many unsung heroes—people who take a great risk or make a personal sacrifice for the benefit of another.

Epaphroditus is one of the unsung heroes of the Bible. While you've heard of Moses, David, John, and Paul, chances are you've never heard a sermon preached on Epaphroditus. When I first stumbled upon his story, I was amazed that I'd never heard more about him, for he is commended for many noble attributes. Paul claims Epaphroditus was "a true brother, a faithful worker, and a courageous soldier" (verse 25). He cared deeply for people and was sensitive to their concerns (verse 26). He even risked his life in order to contribute to the work of Christ (verse 30). If Paul could have, I think he would have awarded Epaphroditus the equivalent of a Purple Heart.

A true hero is anyone who counts the high cost of helping another and decides to pay that price, regardless of the outcome. Chen is such a hero, proclaimed to be a "guardian angel." His story appeared in the September 21, 2004, edition of the *Chicago Tribune*:

> The Yangtze River Bridge, a national landmark in China, is always crowded with traffic, while the great river 100 yards below is filled with barges. The bridge also has thousands of pedestrians, so it is not easy to spot those determined to jump. Over 1,000 people have jumped since the bridge opened in 1968. A man who works on the bridge observed, "It's a place that has a 100 percent success rate."
>
> In 2003, Chen, a man in his mid-30s, became a self-appointed guardian angel, coming to the bridge every weekend to try to stop people from jumping. He counts 42 people whom he has stopped from committing suicide, talking some down and wrestling with others. He has also had five people slip from his grasp to their deaths…
>
> Asked how he can identify potential jumpers from the sea of people, Chen answers, "It is very easy to recognize. A person who walks without spirit."
>
> Chen has gained some attention in the press and now several college students help him patrol the bridge, as do a few people

whom he has saved from jumping. "We have to teach people to love life and treasure life," Chen says.[1]

Chen has the heart of an evangelist and the spirit of a hero. He says, "If I save one person, one is a lot." What an extraordinary example for Christians to consider.

While we may not have a dangerous bridge to patrol, we can save others from eternal death. Like Chen, we may find ourselves in a wrestling match with some who seem determined to perish. We may eventually lose some from heaven's grasp, but we may very well save numerous souls, giving the gift of new life here on earth as well as eternal life in paradise.

Being someone's spiritual hero may require a significant investment. Are you willing to spend time in prayer for someone other than yourself or your immediate family and friends? Are you willing to petition God for someone that the rest of the church considers "beyond help"? Are you willing to invest enormous amounts of energy serving or speaking with someone who may not ever see theological things your way, simply because God loves him or her like crazy?

Granted, these are costly investments. But doesn't being a spiritual hero and impacting someone's life for all eternity make the cost a relatively small price to pay? I think so, especially when I envision meeting that person in heaven someday, basking in the presence of the loving God I've led them to.

HOLDING HIS HAND

Am I willing to be inconvenienced in order to reach out to others with the saving message of the gospel, or do I consider the cost of evangelism too high? Why?

_____

_____

_____

If I succeed in saving someone from eternal death, how will I feel? How might God reward my evangelistic efforts?

_____

_____

_____

If I don't succeed in bringing someone to Christ, do I believe God will still reward me for trying? Can I leave the results up to Him and simply do all I can to help others?

_____

_____

_____

> *Almighty God,*
>
> *We are all standing on a bridge, either waiting to cross over to spend eternity with You or considering a lethal jump into the depths of eternal separation from You. Help us to be on the lookout for our brothers and sisters who have strayed from Your path and to use our evangelistic efforts to lead them back to You. In Jesus' name. Amen.*

MAXIMIZE YOUR MOMENT

Daily reading: Acts 15:22–17:15; 1 Thessalonians 1:1–7

Key passage: We know that God loves you, dear brothers and sisters, and that he chose you to be his own people. For when we brought you the Good News, it was not only with words but also with power, for the Holy Spirit gave you full assurance that what we said was true. And you know that the way we lived among you was further proof of the truth of our message. So you received the message with joy from the Holy Spirit in spite of the severe suffering it brought you. In this way, you imitated both us [Paul, Silas, and Timothy] and the Lord. As a result, you yourselves became an example to all the believers in Greece. (1 Thessalonians 1:4–7)

---

*I*f you are like me, when you hear the name *Silas*, you immediately think about the dynamic duo of Paul and Silas—kind of like Batman and Robin or the Lone Ranger and Tonto. But how much do we really know about Silas and all that God did through him in the early church? Check out his impressive spiritual resume: Silas was…

1. One of two distinguished leaders chosen by the apostles, elders, and church members as a delegate to Syria with Paul and Barnabas, delivering the important decree of the Jerusalem council (Acts 15:22).

2. A prophet who spoke to Christians with powerful words of encouragement and strength (Acts 15:32).

3. Chosen by Paul to be his traveling companion throughout Syria and Cilicia (Acts 15:40).

4. Paul's co-laborer on his second missionary journey to Derbe and Lystra, along with Timothy (Acts 16:1).

5. A minister to the people of Corinth for one-and-a-half years (Acts 18:11; 2 Corinthians 1:19).

6. Likely a respected Christian scribe.[1] Based on the opening verses, Silas penned both letters to the Thessalonian church (1 Thessalonians 1:1; 2 Thessalonians 1:1).

7. Peter's helper when he wrote his first book (1 Peter 5:12).

8. A victim of hardships along with Paul at Philippi, Thessalonica, and Berea, including physical torture and imprisonment (Acts 16:16–24; 17:5–6, 13–15).

9. Alongside Paul when he preached the good news in many other regions such as Phrygia, Galatia, Mysia, and Macedonia.[2]

10. Trustworthy. When Paul left for Athens, Silas remained in Macedonia with Timothy to help supervise the work they'd begun in that region (Acts 17:14).

Over and over we see Silas being "chosen"—chosen to be a penman, prophet, and preacher as well as a missionary, manager, and martyr. Obviously, Paul and other believers had great confidence in this man's capabilities, as they gave him more and more responsibility along the way.

But we never see Silas complaining about all the responsibilities piled on him. He never uses excuses to resist going into a new region as an ambassador of Christ. The words "not my job" do not appear to be in his vocabulary. He doesn't pack up and go home because he's had enough persecution. He perseveres at every turn. He stands firm alongside Paul with every ounce of courage and conviction anyone could muster. Never was the spread of the gospel so vital as during the times of Paul's missionary journeys, and Silas wasn't going to miss his opportunity to do all he could for the glory of God. He was determined to maximize his moment in history.

Jackson Rogers is another person who maximized his opportunity to do all he could for God's glory. As a nine-year-old member of First Presbyterian Church of San Antonio, Jackson accepted his pastor's challenge to take one hundred dollars and do something good for someone. Many other congregants accepted the challenge as well, agreeing to report back to the church how they used the money.

Jackson felt compelled to help homeless people, but he didn't want to just hand the money over to a street person or even to a shelter. He wanted to maximize his opportunity. Brainstorming with his dad for several weeks, Jackson decided to spend the one hundred dollars on paper and stamps, and then embarked on a letter-writing campaign to raise money to cover the cost of one house through Habitat for Humanity. With a total price tag of fifty thousand dollars, Jackson had no idea how much he could raise, but he sent letters to two hundred people on faith that he could at least multiply his initial amount. The *San Antonio Express-News* reported that Jackson's efforts were completely irresistible to one woman, who gave him an unexpected boost:

> A woman was so touched by his letter that she passed it on. Soon, people from Tennessee, Virginia, and Idaho were sending in checks. The 170 people who responded made the effort worthwhile, contributing $43,000. When the congregation at First Presbyterian learned the little miracle-worker was $7,000 short of his goal, it chipped in the rest.[3]

Because Jackson Rogers maximized his moment to do something great for God and to help others, Stephanie Ramirez and her family now reside in "the house that Jack built" before he was even ten years old.

Silas and Jackson both illustrate that regardless of how young or old we are, regardless of how much education we have, regardless of the resources that are available to us, we can make a difference in people's lives if we're simply willing to maximize our moments.

HOLDING HIS HAND

When given opportunities within my church or community to help other people, what is my attitude? Do I avoid getting involved because that's "not my job," or do I seek to maximize my moments to bring glory to God?

_____

_____

_____

What is one evangelistic or humanitarian opportunity before me right now that would allow me to maximize my moment, bring glory to God, and show someone His extravagant love?

_____

_____

_____

What do I need to do in order to make sure I maximize this moment?

_____

_____

_____

Father God,

Forbid it that we would allow our complacency to prevent us from maximizing our moment! Give us eyes to recognize the needs in this world, ears to listen for Your guidance, and a heart to make a difference in people's lives. Amen.

Keep Unusual Company

Daily reading: Mark 2:13–17

Key passage: But when some of the teachers of religious law who were Pharisees saw him eating with people like that, they said to his disciples, "Why does he eat with such scum?"

When Jesus heard this, he told them, "Healthy people don't need a doctor—sick people do. I have come to call sinners, not those who think they are already good enough." (Mark 2:16–17)

*N*either Jesus nor Matthew worried about their image or their reputation or what the neighbors would say about who they were hanging out with. I love that Matthew felt the freedom to invite tax collectors and notorious sinners into his home and that Jesus preferred to socialize with the sinners over the saints. This made His message all the more inviting to those who felt unworthy of God's redeeming love.

I recently spoke at a church where I discovered this same attitude, even in the youth. I was giving my testimony at Celebration Fellowship in Fort Worth, Texas, talking about the loose lifestyle I lived as a teenager. Yet I didn't get the typical "deer in the headlights" look, nor were the kids whispering to each other in disbelief that I was being so open and honest about it. They just smiled and nodded, as if this was something they heard every Sunday.

After the seminar I commented to the pastor, Dr. James Reeves, about how maturely these teens handled the topic of sexual integrity. He said, "Oh, they hear this kind of stuff frequently. Actually, many of their parents are recovering sex addicts."

"And they *know* this about their parents?" I inquired, surprised.

"Oh yes!" he replied. "We have a unique church concept here. We aren't your typical country club church. We consider ourselves a 'hospital church.'"

James went on to tell me how this church concept evolved. As a senior pastor in his midthirties, all his emotional bills began coming due. Unresolved issues from his painful childhood (growing up poor with an abusive, alcoholic father and a Jehovah's Witnesses mother) continued to haunt him, and he spiraled into a deep depression that robbed him of sleep, weight, and the ability to function. He tried to follow the church's standard advice to just pray, study, serve, give, and love Jesus more, but that prescription failed miserably. He did love Jesus and followed these spiritual disciplines every day, but he still felt as if he were dying. Then he had a major revelation as to why.

James explains, "I couldn't talk about what was happening to me because my church wasn't a safe place for anyone to be honest about their problems, especially not the senior pastor. I came to realize that I had three options: (1) continue as I was and probably die; (2) leave the ministry and try to figure my life out; or (3) try to change the church into the kind of place where hurting people like me could find help, hope, and healing. It was change or die. Fortunately, we chose to change.

It's been fifteen years since James realized that the Great Physician, Jesus, needed a hospital in which to do His work—a safe place where people could tell their secrets and experience emotional and spiritual healing in the context of a caring and supportive community of faith. Celebration Fellowship sees itself as a hospital for the hurting rather than a club for the initiated. "You can reach out your arms on any Sunday and touch all kinds of recovering addicts around you—sex and porn addicts, alcoholics, and narcotics abusers. They all find help, healing, and hope here among us," James proudly explains.

Indeed, emotional wounds know absolutely no tax bracket, social standing, or educational boundaries. Everyone from doctors and lawyers to blue-collar workers and homeless people needs healing from emotional wounds. Have you experienced healing from the emotional wounds you have suffered in life? If so, are you actively helping others to experience healing as well? This is how we can live a truly irresistible life—by modeling wholeness and emulating the care and compassion that Jesus has for the broken.

James went on to say, "We don't just tolerate the hurting. We actively seek them out and invite them in. We go into the highways and byways and search for them. We believe that is the clearest expression of the strategy of Jesus Himself, and more clearly reflects His heart than anything else we could be or do."

Indeed, the Great Physician came to heal those who are sick, not to rub elbows with those who have their act together. We are all sick at some level and at some point in our lives, and we all need both His emotional and spiritual healing. If you are ready to care less about your image and reputation and more about healing the emotionally wounded in our world, then you are on the threshold of living a truly irresistible life.

HOLDING HIS HAND

How would I feel about attending a church where I could stretch out my hands and touch recovering addicts all around me? Why?

_____

_____

_____

_____

What does it mean to be a "safe place" for spiritual strugglers? Has anyone ever been such a place for me? What did that person do to make me feel safe?

_____

_____

_____

_____

How might God be able to work through me if I overcome any fears I have of such hurting people and embrace my role as an assistant to the Great Physician?

_____

_____

_____

_____

Almighty God,

We acknowledge that You didn't send Your Son just to rub elbows with the saints, but to bring hope and healing to sinners' lives. We thank You for the hope and healing You've given to us, and we pray that Your Holy Spirit will inspire us to reach out to others with the same care, concern, and compassion You've always had for us. Amen.

Restore Life

Daily reading: John 11:1–44

Key passage: So the two sisters sent a message to Jesus telling him, "Lord, the one you love is very sick."

But when Jesus heard about it he said, "Lazarus's sickness will not end in death. No, it is for the glory of God. I, the Son of God, will receive glory from this." (John 11:3–4)

---

*L*azarus is very sick. That one sentence catapulted Jesus into action, not to run and save Lazarus *before* he died, but *after* he died. By bringing Lazarus back from the dead, Jesus demonstrated not only His power over death, but also His passion for protecting and restoring life.

Bev Kline of Tyler, Texas, also has a passion for protecting and restoring life, and was catapulted into action to save lives by one sentence as well. In 1982 a troubled teenager told Bev, "I think I'm pregnant."

When the teen approached her, everything within Bev wanted to help—not just with a pat on the back and a prayer for guidance, but with practical help and spiritual support. When she phoned the public-health department to inquire about a free pregnancy test, she was given a toll-free phone number through which women could obtain such a test. After the test was performed, Bev phoned for the results. The girl was indeed pregnant. Then the operator suggested, "If she'll get her boyfriend to give her $300 and then drive to Dallas on Saturday, we'll solve the problem."

Bev knew that aborting the unborn baby would result in the loss of a child and also take a spiritual toll on the young woman's life. How did Bev know? Because before she came to Christ, she had two abortions herself. Bev knew that postabortive women have thoughts that haunt them the rest of their lives, and that this girl, if she chose this route, would have thoughts such as, *How could God forgive me for killing my own child? How could I forgive myself? And how will I ever face my baby in heaven after robbing him/her of any chance at life?* When Bev advised the young woman not to abort the child, she responded, "I won't have an abortion if I can find a place to stay. I have nowhere to go."

Bev welcomed the pregnant teen into her own home. Suspecting other women were also responding to the ploy of the free pregnancy test, Bev also purchased her first batch of tests. Then she spread the word around the medical community in her town that they didn't have to refer women to the abortion clinic in Dallas anymore because she was offering free pregnancy tests in Tyler. This was the beginning of Living Alternatives Ministries.

Within twenty minutes of plugging in the phone dedicated to the ministry, Bev received calls from six women needing help. Within a month, she was drowning in the overwhelming needs of so many women. Bev says, "I was amazed by the opportunity to share Christ through the simple offer of a free pregnancy test." Where the abortion clinic saw the request for a pregnancy test as the sale of an abortion, Bev saw the request as an invitation to hear the good news of Jesus Christ. She says, "When a girl asks for the test, she is basically asking, 'Do you know where I can find love?' and in that moment, there is opportunity to minister to her physically, emotionally, and spiritually. She is wide open to hear all about salvation, forgiveness, sexual purity, and healthy choices."

Within a year of starting Living Alternatives, Bev was able to purchase a four-bedroom house that had been gutted by fire for only $15,000. Local churches got involved and helped renovate the home, donating thousands of dollars worth of materials and labor. Six young women moved into the Tyler facility, and it remained at full capacity over the next several years. Then in 1990, through a series of logistical and financial miracles, God provided Living Alternatives with a sprawling 10,000-square-foot home on 40 acres of beautiful land—enough to house twenty women and several full-time staff!

In spite of the persecution she has faced from pro-choice advocates, hospital workers, and the legal system over the past twenty-five years, Bev has labored to live an irresistible, grace-filled life, drawing pregnant girls toward God's extravagant love. Under the Living Alternatives umbrella, she has launched numerous ministries including the Pregnancy Resource Center, Fatherheart Maternity Home, Loving Alternatives (an adoption service to help place babies in permanent homes), Eagle Charter School (which gives residents an opportunity to continue in their studies while living in the maternity home), and an aftercare program that offers abstinence education, discipleship, Bible studies, and parenting classes (for those who choose to raise their own babies). Through these programs, Bev has pulled together hundreds of volunteers and given thousands of women, babies, and adoptive families great hope for their future. She has also taught others across the nation how to establish such ministries in their local communities.

As an unmarried woman who has never given birth, Bev says, "I can identify with the barren woman in Isaiah 54 who must enlarge her tents for the children God will bring. I look forward to seeing my two babies in heaven someday, but until then, God has many for me to care for. This isn't a sacrifice, however, but a privilege and a joy to give my life back to my heavenly Bridegroom through the ministries of Living Alternatives."

Just as Jesus gave Lazarus a second chance at life, every child Bev saves from abortion is a testimony to Jesus' redemptive and restorative power. Indeed, I can only imagine how many individuals will come to hug Bev in heaven to say, "Thank you for loving Jesus without limits and for saving my life."

HOLDING HIS HAND

What does Lazarus's second chance at life say about the God who raised him from the dead? Why did Jesus raise him?

_____

_____

_____

What does a child who is saved from abortion say about the God who gives life? Why might God want to see children live rather than be aborted?

_____

_____

_____

Is there some painful experience in my past that prompts me to want to help others avoid or overcome that same pain? If so, what?

_____

_____

_____

> _Father God,_
>
> _Thank You for desiring to give each of Your children life in abundance. Show us how we can help others live a more abundant life, especially by avoiding some of the mistakes that we are painfully familiar with. You alone can take the lemons we've picked for ourselves and turn them into sweet lemonade. In Jesus' name. Amen._

DO AS THE ROMANS DO

Daily reading: 1 Corinthians 9

Key passage: When I am with the Jews, I become one of them so that I can bring them to Christ. When I am with those who follow the Jewish laws, I do the same, even though I am not subject to the law, so that I can bring them to Christ. When I am with the Gentiles who do not have the Jewish law, I fit in with them as much as I can. In this way, I gain their confidence and bring them to Christ. But I do not discard the law of God; I obey the law of Christ.

When I am with those who are oppressed, I share their oppression so that I might bring them to Christ. Yes, I try to find common ground with everyone so that I might bring them to Christ. I do all this to spread the Good News, and in doing so I enjoy its blessings. (1 Corinthians 9:20–23)

I was thirty-four years old when our family went on our first mission trip outside of the United States. Our destination was Omoa, Honduras, in Central America. Our mission was to bless a struggling all-girls orphanage with several construction projects and to teach vulnerable young women how to look for love in all the right places.

I knew we would face major challenges as we tried to exist far outside our comfort zone. For an entire month a tiny one-bedroom dwelling with two full-size mattresses would be home to our family—a six-foot-seven husband who has to sleep diagonally on anything smaller than a king-size bed, a wife who gets crabby when sleep-deprived, a ten-year-old daughter who is used to having her own private room, and a seven-year-old son with ADHD who would have no friends, television, or Nintendo to occupy his time during our four-week stay.

Still, none of these challenges fazed me nearly as much as the tidbit of information I received the night before we left on our journey. Our group leader announced, "Ladies, leave your makeup bags at home." *What? Surely she's kidding!* I thought. My vanity wanted to protest, but fortunately someone else beat me to it and asked why we couldn't take makeup. "We'll be residing in a primitive part of the country where people are far too poor to afford luxuries such as makeup. The only women who wear it are the prostitutes, and you don't want anyone mistaking you for a lady of the night." Suddenly the request made perfect sense, and the famous admonition came to mind. "When in Rome, do as the Romans do." I left my makeup bag at home.

"When I am with the Jews, I become one of them.... When I am with the Gentiles who do not have the Jewish law, I fit in with them as much as I can" (verses 20–21). Paul's words might lead some to accuse him of being a fickle, two-faced, double-minded fence-sitter. What was the reason for his chameleon-like behavior? To win others to Christ.

Paul knew he needed to blend in with others in order to gain their trust and friendship. If he insisted on doing something outside of their cultural norm, exercising his rights to do as he pleased regardless of others' expectations, some might turn against him. How could their hearts be won for Christ if they were hardened toward His messenger for some petty reason? Paul wasn't being wishy-washy; he was being wise.

We need to exercise similar wisdom when it comes to dealing with people outside of our own culture. In the aforementioned situation I could have proudly insisted, "I don't go anywhere without my makeup. They'll just have to deal with it." But would the young women I was speaking to have opened their hearts to God if they had thought I resembled a prostitute? Most likely not. Leaving my makeup bag at home was a small price to pay to win the hearts of these precious girls.

Our family has had to make small sacrifices in every country we've entered as missionaries. In Zimbabwe we were told to dress simply and to avoid jewelry so as not to arouse suspicion. We were served certain foods that were not especially suited to our taste buds, some of which we had to eat with our hands because that's what everyone else did. We just smiled and scooped it up with our fingers, grateful to be a part of the community. As we departed that country two weeks later, the host whispered in my ear that her daughter had remarked, "Mom, these Americans aren't spoiled at all!" I took that as a huge compliment to the work we had accomplished there.

The funniest "when in Rome, do as the Romans do" moment came in the Gamboa Rainforest of Panama. The group Erin and I were with took a boat ride deep into the jungle to spend the day with a tribe. We were greeted by men along the shore who were wearing little more than a G-string. As we followed them into their large meeting hut, some topless women greeted us. Of course, these tribal people did not expect us to strip our T-shirts off or exchange our shorts for G-strings, but they did expect us to join them in their festive dance—a dance in which we were to walk around in a circle together flapping our arms wide like an eagle in flight. As I flapped my arms, I'd occasionally bump into the topless woman behind me, and I was too afraid to turn around to see what part of her almost-naked body I had bumped. I just kept flapping, dancing, and laughing hysterically together with everyone else.

On this particular trip to Panama, the group we were with was so large that the only place big enough to house us all together was a five-star resort hotel. I thought it was heaven! We were out all day in the hot sun doing dramas and street evangelism, but then got to come back to comfy rooms and hot meals prepared by world-renowned chefs. I asked my daughter, "Isn't this the life?"

Erin responded, "Mom, I wish we were staying in the village huts or even in the streets with the homeless people."

Shocked, I asked, "Why in the world would you rather be out there than right here in this paradise?"

"Because out there is where the people are, and I don't feel as connected to them when I have to leave them every day to come to a place like this." I was incredibly humbled by my thirteen-year-old's heart. She was in Rome, and she wanted to do as the Romans do, not as the rich tourists do.

Of course, you don't have to be in a foreign country to recognize the need for flexibility in winning others to Christ. Sometimes it's simply a matter of getting a pulse for where a particular person or group of people are spiritually, emotionally, mentally, politically, socially, and economically. Are they mature Christians or baby Christians? Are they younger and energetic or older and more serene? Are they radically charismatic in their approach to worship or more traditional and formal? Are they members of the Ivy League or the hometown bowling league? Did they grow up with silver spoons or soup-kitchen spoons in their mouths? You get the idea. Test the waters. Tactfully take a reading of their cultural temperature. Then do as the Romans do so that you, like Paul, can win them to Christ.

HOLDING HIS HAND

If someone from a foreign country came here to witness to me, yet disapproved of my American cultural norms, how would it impact me? Would I be open to what they had to say? Why or why not?

_____

_____

_____

While I would never want to break God's laws in order to fit in, am I willing to be flexible around people who live in a different culture than what I am accustomed to so that I can witness to them about God's unconditional love? Why or why not?

_____

_____

_____

God of all nations, tribes, and tongues,

Thank You for the opportunities You give us to win others for Christ—both those around the globe and those just around the block. Help us to be sensitive to the cultural norms and spiritual temperature of others, and show us how to do as others do so that their hearts will be opened to us, and ultimately to You. Amen.

REFUSE TO REMAIN CAPTIVE

Daily reading: Galatians 4:8–19

Key passage: Before you Gentiles knew God, you were slaves to so-called gods that do not even exist. And now that you have found God (or should I say, now that God has found you), why do you want to go back again and become slaves once more to the weak and useless spiritual powers of this world? (Galatians 4:8–9)

---

*I*magine being held against your will, forced into prostitution by brothel owners. Day after day you are used and abused by one man after another. Then one day a man shows up, not to use you but to usher you into a new life. He offers to purchase your freedom from your captors. A deal is made, and suddenly you are free to walk out of that horrendous situation and to pursue a new life. Let me ask you this: *would you even consider remaining?*

Of course, we can't imagine choosing to remain in a life of slavery once we've been set free, but according to Nicholas Kristof, a *New York Times* reporter, that is what some prostitutes in Cambodia do. Kristof wrote about how he purchased the freedom of two prostitutes from their brothel owners.

He chose these women because they were being held against their will, consented to tell their story, and claimed to want to leave prostitution. Kristof purchased the first woman, Srey Neth, for $150. However, the brothel owners demanded more money for the second one, Srey Mom, and her own reluctance made the deal almost impossible to execute. In a story called "Bargaining for Freedom" that appeared in the *New York Times*, Kristof explains:

> After some grumpy negotiation, the owner accepted $203 as the price for Srey Mom's freedom. But then Srey Mom told me that she had pawned her cellphone and needed $55 to get it back.
>
> "Forget about your cellphone," I said. "We've got to get out of here."
>
> Srey Mom started crying. I told her that she had to choose her cellphone or her freedom, and she ran back to her tiny room in the brothel and locked the door....
>
> With Srey Mom sobbing in her room and refusing to be freed without her cellphone, the other prostitutes—her closest friends— began pleading with her to be reasonable. So did the brothel's owner.
>
> "Grab this chance while you can," the owner begged Srey Mom. But the girl would not give in.

Srey Mom only stopped crying when Kristof agreed to buy back the cellphone too. Then she asked for her pawned jewelry to be part of the deal.

Kristof reflected upon the complex emotions making the decision to leave the brothel so difficult. "I have purchased the freedom of two human beings so I can return them to their villages. But will emancipation help them? Will their families and villages accept them? Or will they, like some other girls rescued from sexual servitude, find freedom so unsettling that they slink back to slavery in the brothels? We'll see."[1]

This story vividly illustrates how many people deal with the idea of freedom. Some find it so unfamiliar that they choose to remain in the bondage they're accustomed to. Others return shortly after emancipation. This may explain why many of the Israelites campaigned for a quick return to Egypt, even after God delivered them from backbreaking slave labor. He had promised to usher them into a spacious land of their own, "a land flowing with milk and honey" (Exodus 3:8). However, once out from under Egyptian rule, the Israelites found freedom uncomfortable, unnatural. They had to make decisions for themselves. They had to look to God for guidance. There wasn't anyone in their face barking out orders anymore. They weren't sure how to act. So they began longing to return—longing for familiarity, even though their familiar lifestyle stunk.

Paul warned the Galatians of a similar dynamic, hoping to encourage them to refuse to return to their old lifestyle. He had preached the gospel of grace to set them free from legalism. He had introduced them to the one true God in order to dispel the myth that their pagan gods could do anything for them. Through Paul's preaching, they had come to know God in an intimate and personal way. Yet in today's reading we see Paul pleading with the Galatians not to become slaves to legalism and false gods once more.

Why did Paul feel the need to write these words? Because the Galatians were backsliding into bondage. As much as he wanted people to abide by God's laws, he didn't want them depending upon their acts of righteousness and observance of religious occasions for their salvation. He wanted them to understand that salvation comes by grace through faith in Jesus Christ alone.

Of course, we'll always wrestle with sin as long as we're alive, but we discount grace and dishonor God when we wallow in sin instead of wrestle with it. How can we draw others toward God's love and transforming power if we aren't trying to live a transformed life? We need an attitude like that of the evangelist Billy Sunday, who said:

> Listen, I'm against sin. I'll kick it as long as I've got a foot. I'll fight it
> as long as I've got a fist. I'll butt it as long as I've got a head. And I'll
> bite it as long as I've got a tooth, and when I'm old, fistless, footless

and toothless, I'll gum it till I go home to glory and it goes home to perdition.[2]

When we refuse to return to a lifestyle that discounts grace or dishonors God, our lives become a testimony of Christ's transformation power. This was certainly true for my step-grandfather, Sparky. When I recognized my bondage to dysfunctional romantic relationships in my late twenties, I confided in very few people outside of my Sex & Love Addicts Anonymous (SLAA) group. But I knew I could confide in Sparky, so I did. While I was growing up, Sparky would tell me every year that he was celebrating another "birthday"—not a biological birthday, but a spiritual and emotional one. It was his Alcoholics Anonymous anniversary. Although he'd made a mess of the first half of his life, Sparky refused to return to alcohol in the last half of his life, and he was a much better man for it. His commitment to remaining free from such bondage truly inspired me to get free and stay free from my own addictive behavior as well.

Refuse to remain captive, girlfriend. Regardless of what you have been enslaved to in the past, know that you will automatically draw others toward God's extravagant love as you refuse to return to that sin and live the overcomer's lifestyle that is your free gift through Jesus Christ.

HOLDING HIS HAND

Are there things I've done or ways I've behaved in my past that seriously damaged my Christian witness at the time (for example, lying, cheating, stealing, gossiping, or engaging in addictive behaviors)? If so, what were those things?

_____

_____

_____

_____

Am I choosing to remain captive? If not, how has Jesus Christ set me free from these sins?

_____

_____

_____

_____

How will refusing to return to that sin(s) enhance my effectiveness as an evangelist?

_____

_____

_____

_____

Precious Lord Jesus,

*Thank You for paying the price to give us complete freedom
from spiritual bondage. Help us remain free from our
slavery to sin. And as we live an overcomer's lifestyle, help
others recognize that Your transformation power is genuine
and available to all who seek it. Amen.*

TURN MISERY
INTO MINISTRY

Daily reading: Romans 5:1–11

Key passage: We can rejoice, too, when we run into problems and trials, for we know that they are good for us—they help us learn to endure. And endurance develops strength of character in us, and character strengthens our confident expectation of salvation. And this expectation will not disappoint us. For we know how dearly God loves us, because he has given us the Holy Spirit to fill our hearts with his love. (Romans 5:3–5)

When I first met my husband in 1989, we were in a singles' Sunday-school class together. We were asked what our favorite passage of Scripture was, and Greg began reciting Romans 5:3–5 about how we are to "rejoice" in our sufferings. He correlated this verse to every dark cloud having a silver lining. As an example, he told of how he had been mercilessly picked on as an exceptionally tall but incredibly uncoordinated kid. People called him "String Bean," "Toothpick," and "Giraffe" without consideration for his feelings. Because of these experiences, however, Greg invested a great deal of his spare time as an adult counselor with the youth group, hoping to enhance the self-esteem of other young men. At the time he counted this volunteer work as one of his greatest blessings in life.

Chances are, most of us have early life experiences that bring painful memories to mind. As adults, we must decide what we are going to do with these experiences, emotions, and energy. As one of my counselors used to say, "We can choose a bitter land or a better land." We can wallow in our misery, or we can turn it into a ministry, as Kayla is doing.

I met Kayla in 2006 when she came to Garden Valley, Texas, to be an intern with Teen Mania's Honor Academy. As we walked and talked one morning, I was stunned to hear what kind of suffering this girl had endured throughout most of her life—suffering that had produced remarkable perseverance, character, and expectation of how God could use her to bless others who'd suffered similar circumstances.

Kayla was born three months early to a mother who was high on crack cocaine. When Kayla was two years old, she and her younger brother were taken from their biological mother and placed in the custody of their aunt for a short time; then later they went from foster home to foster home every few years. Their caretakers were often emotionally, mentally, and sometimes physically abusive, and she remembers desperately trying to cover for her brother's typical "little boy mischief" so that he would not get beaten the way she often did. Kayla also had food withheld from her as a "corrective measure."

When she was eight, Kayla and her brother were placed into two different foster homes. Kayla became severely depressed without her brother by her side. She was placed on antidepressants and several other medications so that she wouldn't have to be dealt with.

The next stop for Kayla would be a treatment center for children who suffer from RAD (Reactive Attachment Disorder), or who have a difficult time bonding with others. While there she was devastated to receive the news that her brother had been killed in a car accident. Kayla's life's purpose had been bound up in taking care of her brother. She began to question what use God could possibly have for her. Rather than turning to more medications to numb her pain, however, she turned to God's Word instead. She purchased her first Bible at age eleven and began diligently reading up to ten chapters per day, hoping to find answers to her many "Why?" questions.

Kayla was sent to yet another foster home, before she was finally adopted by the next family she lived with. A month later she gave her life to the Lord, although many of her questions about her life's purpose remained unanswered.

A few summers later, Kayla went on a mission trip to Peru, where she sensed God saying to her, *I know you are hurting over the loss of your brother, Kayla, but embrace your brokenness. It's what motivates you to serve Me so passionately.*

Kayla's past miseries have inspired her dreams of developing a ministry to orphaned children. "The Lord has given me a passion for this lost and hurting generation," Kayla says. "He has placed it on my heart to have a group home for foster kids and to work with the homeless to alleviate their suffering and give them a hope for their future. I cannot turn my back on my past just because I was miraculously blessed with an adoptive family. I must use my experiences to reach out to weary and broken children so they can see there is hope."

Sadly, there are overwhelming numbers of weary and broken children in the United States alone. One out of every four people standing in a soup-kitchen line is a child.[1] Young people have only a 50 percent chance of escaping poverty.[2] Twenty thousand orphans turn eighteen every year and are released from the foster-care system, often without job training, proper housing, or sufficient life skills.[3]

Of course, when we look outside this country into far less privileged regions of the world, the numbers of homeless children are astounding. As Jesus said, "The harvest is so great, but the workers are so few" (Matthew 9:37). Jesus went on to encourage His disciples, "So pray to the Lord who is

in charge of the harvest; ask him to send more workers for his fields"
(Matthew 9:38).

Kayla has prayed that prayer and has since recognized that she is the
worker who is to go out into the fields. Why? To live an irresistible life as an
overcomer of her difficult circumstances. Kayla rejoices over how her trials
have helped her develop perseverance, character, and hope, and she wants to
teach others how to do the same.

HOLDING HIS HAND

What kind of miseries have I experienced?

_____

_____

_____

How might God turn my misery into my ministry?

_____

_____

_____

> *Lord God,*
>
> *Although our past painful experiences broke Your heart as
> well, we thank You for being a God who can take our mis-
> eries and turn them into life-transforming ministries! Give
> us the courage to be real with others, so that we can give
> them even greater glimpses into Your lavish redemptive love
> for Your people. Amen.*

BRIDGE CULTURAL GAPS

Daily reading: Acts 8:26–40

Key passage: So Philip began with this same Scripture and then used many others to tell him the Good News about Jesus.

As they rode along, they came to some water, and the eunuch said, "Look! There's some water! Why can't I be baptized?" He ordered the carriage to stop, and they went down into the water, and Philip baptized him. (Acts 8:35–38)

*A*t first glance, we may not recognize the magnitude of what took place between the eunuch and Philip on that desert road to Gaza, but this salvation experience was certainly one for the record books and cause for the angels to celebrate! Why? Because the Holy Spirit drew two different individuals together, bridging cultural gaps that had never before been bridged.

What cultural gaps am I referring to? First, understand that Philip was a Jew. Jews had strict rules and regulations about who "belonged" in their religious community and who didn't. Gentiles certainly didn't belong, nor did eunuchs. A eunuch was an officer or public official assigned by a ruler to oversee the women's quarters. So that there was no hanky-panky going on, these men were usually castrated.[1] Eunuchs were excluded from the Jewish religious observances (Deuteronomy 23:1).[2] It was far outside the job description of a "good Jew" for Philip to walk alongside the carriage of a eunuch and talk to him about spiritual matters. Still, the Holy Spirit guided Philip toward the path that this eunuch would be traveling (Acts 8:26).

The eunuch also acted far outside the norm for Gentile behavior. He had just been to Jerusalem to worship and was returning with a copy of the prophecy of Isaiah, which would have been difficult for a Gentile to come by. Most importantly, he was so hungry to understand the prophecy's meaning that he was open to further instruction from a Jew.[3] Following the prompting of the Holy Spirit, Philip walked alongside the eunuch's carriage and offered to explain the prophecy. The eunuch begged Philip to join him in the carriage so they could discuss the matter as teacher and pupil. Soon the eunuch asked Philip to baptize him.

To get an idea of how shocking this was, picture a typical white southerner's reaction to a black man and a white woman dining together in a restaurant in the 1950s. Such behavior was unheard of. Appalling. It would start the rumor mill churning for sure. But God simply doesn't see black and white, male and female, Jew and Gentile (Galatians 3:28). He only sees humans in need of His grace, and so the Holy Spirit brought about this unlikely meeting.

Chris and Nicki Bradshaw understand what it means to follow the leading of the Holy Spirit to bridge cultural gaps. In July 2005 they left their comfortable home and ministry in the Bible Belt of east Texas to journey northward to Royal Oak, Michigan. They walked the city streets, praying about how God might want to use them to impact that community. They soon learned that many people run to Royal Oak because they hear that "the food is good and the partying is excellent." Hedonism seems to be the order of the day. Bars and nightclubs far outnumber churches. Royal Oak prides itself on its tolerant world-view. The unspoken motto on the street is, "Any lifestyle you want to live, you are welcome to live it here!"

As a result, Royal Oak has become a place of community for the gay, lesbian, bisexual, and transgender (GLBT) community. Gay people seek the solace of others in the gay community, often because they've felt so unwelcomed by everyone else. So part of Chris and Nicki's vision for establishing The Oaks Church (www.theoakschurch.net) is to bridge the gap between those who have not yet chosen to follow Jesus with those who have, regardless of the cultural, social, political, racial, or sexual differences that exist between them.

Just as the Holy Spirit moved to connect Philip and the eunuch, He is connecting people from all walks of life at The Oaks Church. Nicki was thrilled to hear one woman say to a lesbian friend, "You should come and check out this church!"

The woman apprehensively responded, "What? You mean *I* can go there?"

"Yes! This is one church you *can* go to," her friend replied.

Another woman told Nicki that she was terribly wounded when a church insisted she had no more than twelve months to renounce and deny all thoughts and feelings she had for another woman, or else she must not be a true believer. Although she'd listened to the Holy Spirit, ran from the relationship, and refused to act on her emotions, she still felt condemned when she found herself still wrestling the urge to call the other woman even after a year's time. Her sanctification deadline had come and gone, and it seemed the church had no more grace or love left for her. Rather than giving her credit for not acting out on her desires, they gave her a spiritual pink slip. They were through with her.

However, this woman has found a compassionate place of refuge and restoration at The Oaks Church. "God doesn't place time limitations on our sanctification process, nor do we," explains Nicki. "We will not abandon a believer in the midst of their pursuit of holiness."

The mission of The Oaks is to create a unique, interactive environment where people can feel loved without fear of judgment or condemnation. Chris and Nicki explain, "There is a way to love people without compromising the gospel. Jesus did it every single day. We are not defying God's truth about the gay lifestyle, but we are speaking the truth while loving gay people and embracing them as children of God so that they'll be encouraged in their journey to know Him personally. After all, the greatest commandment is to love the Lord with all our heart, soul, and mind, and to love our neighbor as ourselves (Matthew 22:37–39). As we grow to love God more, we naturally grow to love others the way He loves them. As we connect more intimately with Jesus, we connect more intimately with one another."

Although Chris and Nicki are seeing fruit from this new ministry, they by no means feel qualified to lead such a church. They remain students at the feet of Jesus. They aren't judgmental and condemning. They seek not to bash the gay lifestyle, but to know people personally and encourage them as they journey to know and follow Jesus.

Are others comfortable sharing their lives with you, regardless of your lifestyle differences? Do they feel loved and respected by you enough to risk judgment? Are they open to your spiritual guidance because they trust that you have their best interest at heart? As we genuinely seek to learn from those who are different from us rather than writing them off, the Holy Spirit can bridge all sorts of cultural gaps. These bridges can become a wonderful avenue through which His extravagant love can flow freely between us and others.

HOLDING HIS HAND

What is my attitude toward those who subscribe to a different cultural lifestyle than one I am accustomed to? Why?

_____

_____

_____

Am I willing to learn from others who are different so that I can be more effective in showing them God's love? Why or why not?

_____

_____

_____

If others feel loved, respected, and accepted by me for who they are, how might that open the door for me to draw them into a more intimate relationship with Christ?

_____

_____

_____

Lord Jesus,

Thank You for accepting us for who we are. Show us how to give others that same acceptance. As we try to love others unconditionally, please send Your Holy Spirit to bridge any cultural gaps that only serve to hinder the spread of the good news about Your saving grace. Amen.

MAKE TIME
FOR OTHERS

Daily reading: Acts 18:18–23; 1 Corinthians 16:5–9

Key passage: This time I don't want to make just a short visit and then go right on. I want to come and stay awhile, if the Lord will let me. (1 Corinthians 16:7)

*I*f we look at how the apostle Paul spent most of his time, we'll recognize that he placed a high priority not just on writing letters, but on the people he was writing to. He wasn't satisfied with sending his penned sentiments via the pony express. He took significant blocks of time and went to great lengths to visit people personally—sailing from Corinth to Syria, then on to Ephesus, Caesarea, Jerusalem, Antioch, Galatia, and Phrygia, as well as many other ports.

Why did he visit all these places? He wasn't on a sightseeing tour. He was on a people-seeing tour. Scripture tells us Paul visited believers in order to encourage them and help them grow in the Lord (Acts 18:23). In Paul's estimation, there was nothing more important than people, and they responded to his message because they felt valued and loved by him.

If we want to draw others toward God's extravagant love, we'll make people a priority as well. Maybe you are thinking, *But I simply can't find time for people!* You are right. It's hard to *find* time. We must *make* time. We all have the same twenty-four hours in a day. It's up to us to use it wisely, and what better investment can we make with our time than to spend a portion of it connecting with other people?

In a culture where we often wear our busyness like a badge of honor, many opportunities for ministering to people's spiritual and emotional needs are lost. If you are a Type-A, driven, always-have-to-be-doing-something personality like me, you may find yourself falling into the trap of filling your to-do list so full of *tasks* that you can't possibly squeeze in *people.* If that's the case, make a section on your to-do list for things that will result in a people connection. For example, mark your calendar to send birthday, anniversary, or friendship cards to let people know you are thinking of them. Next time you plan a grocery-shopping trip close to lunch or dinner, don't grab a burger from a drive-through window; instead call a friend and schedule a one-hour rendezvous at a nearby restaurant. Make it a spontaneous social occasion. When you are penciling in your weekly exercise times, invite a friend to join you for a walk or a trip to the gym. Some of my most intimate times with friends are during pleasant walk-and-talk times. I need to exercise anyway, so it doesn't slow me down to spend an hour connecting heart to heart with someone while walking together.

Speaking of walk-and-talk times, I was recently invited to deliver a series of chapel messages on the campus of Biola University and Talbot School of Theology. On the way there, I was planning to spend my free time in the hotel room, catching up on mounds of paperwork. But then I sensed God saying, *Shannon, I want you to pour out everything you've got into the students on that campus. Come back with nothing left at the end of these three days.* I decided the paperwork could wait until the plane ride home. At the close of my first message, I invited anyone in the student body who desired to meet one-on-one with me to go to the administration building, sign up for a designated thirty-minute time slot, and show up on the track prepared to walk and talk for half an hour. Even though I expected to be drained after spending so much time ministering, that wasn't the case. Proverbs 11:25 is so true—"Those who refresh others will themselves be refreshed."

Of course, some people have needs that we can't conveniently squeeze into our schedule. In those situations, we often have to make a choice—*What comes first, people or tasks?* As the chief of surgery at Waterbury Hospital, Dr. Scott Kurtzman has reason to think his tasks are so important he can't make time for people. However, that's not his philosophy. Here's a summary from a *Reader's Digest* article:

> Dr. Kurtzman was on his way to deliver an 8 a.m. lecture when he witnessed one of the worst crashes in Connecticut history. A dump truck, whose driver had lost control, flipped on its side and skidded into oncoming traffic. The resulting accident involved 20 vehicles; four people died.
>
> Thanks to years of emergency-room experience, Doctor Kurtzman immediately shifted into trauma mode. He worked his way through the mangled mess of people and metal, calling out, "Who needs help?"
>
> After about 90 minutes, when all 16 victims had been triaged and taken to area hospitals, Dr. Kurtzman climbed back into his car, drove to the medical school, and gave his lecture—two hours late.
>
> This was not the first time Dr. Kurtzman has assisted those in need. Over the years, he's stopped at a half-dozen crashes and assisted at three. "A person with my skills simply can't drive by someone who's injured," says Kurtzman. "I refuse to live my life that way."[1]

Of course, we don't have to pull someone from a life-threatening car crash to impact her life in significant ways. Recently I was blessed by a dear neighbor who gave up her Friday night with her family to hang out with me after I had a minor medical procedure. Sharon knew I'd be groggy after the anesthesia and that my husband and kids had to be out of town that night. Instead of sitting by the phone in case I needed her, she decided to sit on my couch and keep me company.

My mother is another person who makes time for others. She always gives her children and grandchildren a "Saturday shopping trip" for their birthdays, not because they are hard to buy for, but because she wants the quality time with them. As nice as it is to pick your own present, the real gift is the time we get to spend with her and the memories we make together.

If you want to draw others toward God's extravagant love, give someone a slice of your precious time. There's no better way to nourish the soul of another and to have your own soul nourished as well.

HOLDING HIS HAND

What are my daily priorities? Do I place people in front of tasks or tasks in front of people? Why?

_____

_____

_____

_____

What does it feel like when people invest their time in me? How does it feel to know I am a priority in their lives?

_____

_____

_____

_____

How can I give someone else the feeling of knowing he or she is important and special to me? When will I do this?

_____

_____

_____

_____

Lord Jesus,

You invested so much of Your time in Your disciples, and now You remain on call for us 24/7! How You must love spending time with Your people! Show us how to enjoy others more. Help us make people a priority in our lives so they will come to know Your love more completely as a result of experiencing our love for them. In Jesus' name. Amen.

FOCUS ON WHAT
MATTERS MOST

Daily reading: Romans 7

Key passage: When we were controlled by our old nature, sinful desires were at work within us, and the law aroused these evil desires that produced sinful deeds, resulting in death. But now we have been released from the law, for we died with Christ, and we are no longer captive to its power. Now we can really serve God, not in the old way by obeying the letter of the law, but in the new way, by the Spirit. (Romans 7:5–6)

Listen to any radio talk show, watch the news on television, or pick up any newspaper or magazine and read for a while. You'll eventually be exposed to the results of some poll where people were asked to respond to certain questions. I'm always hearing about a new Gallup poll, or survey results published by the Barna Group, or Nielsen ratings for television shows. We are a culture obsessed with finding out what everybody else thinks.

It would be interesting to see how people would respond to the question "How does a Christian live?"

I imagine that many who don't understand the Christian life would respond with things such as, "Christians don't smoke or drink or do drugs... they don't go to raunchy movies, adult bookstores, or strip clubs... they don't lie or cheat or steal... they don't go to loud parties or have any fun."

If the pollster replied, "Okay, that's what you think Christians *don't* do. But what are they supposed to do? How do you think they live?" Responses would most likely include, "Go to church, put money in the offering plate, read their Bibles..."

But does God even care about those things? (Already, you may be gasping, thinking *She's committing blasphemy by even suggesting such apostasy!* But before you throw the stone, hear me out.) Does God disqualify the smoker or drinker, the drug abuser, the partier, the stripper, the liar, the cheater, the thief, or even the murderer from spending eternity with Him? Absolutely not. These are people Jesus would be dining with if He were still walking the earth. Why? Because they *need* Him. Their hands are empty of self-righteousness, ready to receive His free gift of grace.

But many Christians already have their hands full of their own self-righteousness, subconsciously thinking, *God's amazing grace is really for the wretched sinners who need it, because I'm doing all the right things.* But is it possible for someone to do all the right things yet still miss altogether what God wants? You bet. The world is full of people who warm the pews most Sundays, pad the offering plates, and even read their Bibles cover to cover. But do they have an intimate relationship with the Author of that Book? Do they recognize their overwhelming need for His grace on a daily (even hourly) basis? No they don't, and there's the problem.

Being a Christian does not mean doing all the "right" things and avoiding all the "wrong" things. Even on our best days, we all fall into sin. There's no way any of us could ever be good enough to merit eternal life on our own. Instead of depending on our works, Christians live in intimate fellowship with Jesus Christ, fully depending on *His* goodness and grace to grant us eternal life.

So when it comes to our efforts to invite others to God's love, we need to ask ourselves if we are trying to disciple people by teaching them to do the right things and avoid the wrong things or if we are drawing them into a deeper relationship with Jesus Christ. Are we focusing on the outside, or are we focusing on what really matters to God—the inside?

In his book *What's So Amazing About Grace?* author Philip Yancey uses the following analogy to paint a vivid picture of what it means to focus on the outside rather than on the inside, and then he responds to that realization:

Samuel Tewk, an English reformer in the nineteenth century, introduced a radical new approach to treatment of the mentally ill. At the time, asylum workers were chaining lunatics to the walls and beating them, in the belief that punishment would defeat the evil forces within. Tewk taught the mentally afflicted how to behave at tea parties and at church. He dressed them the way everyone else was dressed, so that no one would recognize them as mentally ill. On the outside, they looked fine. He did nothing to address their suffering, however, and no matter how they behaved, they remained mentally ill.

One day I realized that I was like one of Tewk's patients; although the church of my childhood had taught me the proper way to behave, and a Bible college had given me more advanced knowledge, neither had cured the deep illness within. Though I had mastered the external behavior, inside the sickness and pain remained. For a time I cast aside the beliefs of my childhood, until God wonderfully revealed himself to me as a God of love and not hate, of freedom and not rules, of grace and not judgment.[1]

How sad that many church leaders and Bible-college professors strain to keep an eagle eye on things such as how short a girl's skirt is or how long a boy's hair is or what part of their bodies are tattooed or pierced, all the while overlooking major problems such as world hunger or stopping the spread of AIDS. If Christians focused more on what really matters and less on what ultimately doesn't, perhaps we'd no longer have reputations that include words like *hypocrite…legalist…goody two-shoes…high and mighty…holier than thou.*

I have to check my heart in this matter frequently. On occasion, a young woman shows up for a counseling appointment looking quite bedraggled. Sometimes I am tempted to ease her pain by treating her to an extreme makeover, replacing her frumpy clothes with a sharp outfit, getting her hair styled so it is no longer hiding her pretty face, and painting her lips and eyes to lighten and brighten them. But then I realize I'd only be hiding her true self behind a cosmetic mask and teaching her that vanity is the answer to her problems. My time and energies are better invested listening to her life story and ministering to the emotional wounds that have driven her toward hiding behind a bad hairstyle and unflattering clothes. Only then will she feel beautiful enough on the inside to allow that beauty to radiate on the outside.

As you seek to attract others to Christianity, remember that you'll never do so by being legalistic about what Christians should and should not do. Forget the rules. Focus on relationships instead. Encourage people to center their lives around what really matters—cultivating a lifestyle of passion and purpose through an intimate relationship with Jesus Christ.

HOLDING HIS HAND

According to today's passage, what is the purpose of the law?

_____

_____

_____

_____

Do I identify with Paul when he said, "In my mind I really want to obey God's law, but because of my sinful nature I am a slave to sin" (Romans 7:25)? Then what is the answer to our sin issues? (See the beginning of verse 25 for the answer.)

_____

_____

_____

_____

As I reach out to others, do I focus on their external behaviors or on their internal condition? Do I promote a list of Christian rules or a loving relationship with our merciful Savior?

_____

_____

_____

_____

Father God,

Thank You for giving us the law, not to bind us, but to show us how amazing Your grace truly is! Because we always fall short of Your perfect holiness, we acknowledge that we are saved only by Your grace. As we draw others toward You, let us focus on the fact that Christianity is not about keeping rigid rules, but about keeping You first in our lives. Amen.

SOW GOOD SEEDS

Daily reading: Galatians 6:1–10

Key passage: Don't be misled. Remember that you can't ignore God and get away with it. You will always reap what you sow! Those who live only to satisfy their own sinful desires will harvest the consequences of decay and death. But those who live to please the Spirit will harvest everlasting life from the Spirit. So don't get tired of doing what is good. Don't get discouraged and give up, for we will reap a harvest of blessing at the appropriate time. (Galatians 6:7–9)

I magine a gardener's surprise if she plants carrots and cucumbers in the spring, then weeks later harvests corn and cantaloupe instead! Can't happen? You're right. It can't. Just as Paul said to the Galatians, we reap what we sow.

Yesterday we talked about the need to focus on the things that matter most rather than on external behaviors. However, according to what Paul says in the above passage, our works *do* matter. Our actions, both positive and negative, will reap corresponding consequences.

So which is it? Do our works matter to God or not?

While salvation is based on faith alone, and God's love toward us is unconditional, He also wants His children to behave appropriately. He wants us to uphold His commandments, for He gave them to us as an expression of His desire to lovingly protect us from the negative effects of sin. God wants us to live righteously—not because that's what earns us favor and eternal life, but because the pursuit of righteousness is the only appropriate response to God's grace and lavish love for us.

Of course, sometimes Christians make bad choices and fail to pursue righteousness. When this happens, we have a prime opportunity to sow good seeds into that person's life instead of seeds of judgment and condemnation. That's what Paul was saying in his closing passage to the Galatians. He exhorts us all to "gently and humbly help that person back onto the right path...share each other's troubles and problems...do what you should [to restore them]" (verses 1–2, 4).

Of course, sowing such seeds often requires confrontation. It usually requires courage. And it *always* requires love. We are not functioning as God's holy watchdogs, but as loving keepers (protectors) of our brothers and sisters. It is only as we speak the truth in love (rather than sweep it under the rug or gossip to others about the matter) that we can truly help others get back on the right path. I once heard it said that "love isn't love until it speaks the truth, and truth isn't truth unless it's spoken in love." In other words, we aren't loving someone when we look the other way. Nor are we speaking the true heart of God by heaping hatred or scorn on them. Sincere love and genuine truth always go hand in hand.

In addition to sowing seeds to help others pursue righteousness, we can also sow good seeds by investing our finances in God's kingdom. While the first half of today's Scripture passage deals with our relationships with other people, the second half deals with our relationship with money. Paul says we have a moral obligation to support the work of Christ by sowing good seeds, which includes giving of our resources to support Christian workers, particularly our pastors and teachers. By tithing regularly to the church, we ensure that the evangelistic work of the church continues.

I'll never forget being approached by a well-meaning member of our church about this topic. This man (I'll call him Nick) was a very successful salesman who drove a BMW and lived in one of the nicest houses in the neighborhood. He pulled my husband and me aside after a Sunday-school lesson on stewardship and said, "I'm not sold on this idea that we have to give of our money. I think as long as we give our time and service to God, the money thing isn't really all that important. Don't you agree?"

Greg and I both swallowed hard in that moment. We didn't want to offend Nick or make him feel stupid, but we didn't want him to continue walking blindly in regard to this issue either. Greg responded, "Actually, what Bob and Kathleen taught today is directly in line with what Jesus taught about money."

Nick looked in my direction as if to say, "What about you? Are you with me on this one?"

I had to speak the truth in love as well, so I added, "Time and service are certainly important, but unfortunately it doesn't keep the lights on, pay the church mortgage, or put food in the pastor's mouth."

Indeed, it takes all of us pooling our resources to keep the church running. Otherwise, it would have to shut its doors. While church is certainly a ministry, it still has to function like any other business. It must be financially supported in order to exist. So it's important for us to sow good seeds into the churches that sow spiritually into us.

According to Paul, pastors and teachers deserve to be paid for their time just like any other worker (Galatians 6:6). One of the best ways we can draw others toward God's extravagant love is by drawing them into a fully functioning church body. A well-trained pastoral staff can minister to the needs of individuals and families in ways that we may not be equipped to on our own. A nice roof overhead and padded seats underneath ensure a pleasant worship experience for all who visit our church. Well-supported missionaries can go places with the gospel that we never dreamed of going. But money is required to provide these things. That money doesn't fall from the sky—it comes out of believers' pockets as an expression of our love for God and our passion for the evangelistic mission He's entrusted to us. As a result of the financial seeds we sow, spiritual fruit blossoms in the life of the church.

Dr. D. James Kennedy tells the story of a man who expressed a concern about money to Peter Marshall, former chaplain of the United States Senate. The man said, "I have a problem. I have been tithing for some time. It wasn't too bad when I was making $20,000 a year. I could afford to give the $2,000. But you see, now I am making $500,000, and there is just no way I can afford to give away $50,000 a year."

Rather than giving advice, Dr. Marshall simply replied, "Yes sir. I see that you do have a problem. I think we ought to pray about it. Is that all right?"

They both bowed their head, and Dr. Marshall boldly prayed, "Dear Lord, this man has a problem, and I pray that you will help him. Lord, reduce his salary back to the place where he can afford to tithe."[1]

As shocking as Dr. Marshall's prayer must have been for this man to hear, I believe he was simply confirming the spiritual laws that Paul wrote about in Galatians 6—we all reap what we sow. If we sow to please our selfish, sinful nature, we harvest decay and destruction. But if we sow to please the Spirit, we will surely harvest many spiritual blessings.

HOLDING HIS HAND

When it comes to confronting a fellow believer, am I prepared to speak the truth in love when necessary? Why or why not?

_____

_____

_____

Do I demonstrate my love for God not just with my time, but with my treasures as well? In what way?

What seeds am I sowing and what type of harvest can I expect to receive from those seeds?

Holy Father,

Help us to recognize the vital roles we play in our church body. Give us the courage to speak the truth in love to our brothers and sisters and the commitment to support the church with our finances. We acknowledge that our relationships and money are ultimately Your gifts to us, so help us sow good seeds by continually offering those gifts back to You. Amen.

LOVE WITHOUT FEAR

Daily reading: 1 John 3:11–24; 4:7–21

Key passage: If we love our Christian brothers and sisters, it proves that we have passed from death to eternal life.... Such love has no fear because perfect love expels all fear. If we are afraid, it is for fear of judgment, and this shows that his love has not been perfected in us. We love each other as a result of his loving us first. (1 John 3:14; 4:18–19)

---

*A*ll of the kids in my youth group were sitting around a bonfire at Beaver's Bend State Park in 1982, talking about our greatest challenges in life. As an immature junior-high-school student, I probably thought my greatest challenge was keeping my face from breaking out after I pigged out on chocolate. I don't remember what I said, but I'll never forget what Stacy Sumrow said: "My greatest challenge is genuinely loving other people."

At that moment, I recall thinking, *That one's easy for me.* Of course, I was thinking of the boyfriend I was gaga over, the best friend that I ate lunch with every day, and the family dog that was always happy to see me.

But in the weeks and months that followed, Stacy's words continued to come to mind, particularly when the older girls would gossip about me on the school bus. Or when boys made fun of my bowlegged walk. Or when my parents' barrage of questions rubbed me the wrong way. *Maybe I was wrong about how easy it is for me to love people,* I thought.

As an adult, I've become painfully aware of how difficult it is to love people—not just those I'd classify as enemies (such as radical terrorists), but those I am closest to (such as family members and church friends). Stacy was right. That which God calls us to do above all else is hardest to do on a consistent basis. I constantly remind myself that love isn't a feeling. It's a commitment to put the person's interests above my own selfish desires.

Of course, the greatest example of such love is Jesus laying down His life for us. When He chose the cross, Christ decided to put my spiritual needs above His personal comfort. I'm sure there were a million things He'd rather have done that weekend than be tortured; suffer a slow, painful death; and be placed in a dark grave. But ultimately, there was nothing more important to Him than accomplishing that which His suffering and death accomplished—eternal life for you and for me. His love was so perfect it overcame any fear of what He was about to undergo.

If you are like me, you want to be able to love like that—to love people completely without fear of what it may cost you. In the book *The Irresistible Revolution,* Shane Claiborne explains how the city of Philadelphia passed legislation making it illegal for homeless people to sleep or ask for money in its public parks. Officials even went so far as to ban all food from the parks so that the homeless population would no longer seek handouts there.

However, many Christians in Philadelphia (the City of Brotherly Love) refused to abide by these new laws. They refused to let their fear of legal consequences prevent them from expressing their love for the homeless. Claiborne writes:

> About a hundred of us gathered in Love Park with homeless friends. We worshiped, sang, and prayed. Then we served communion, which was illegal. But with clergy and city officials there supporting us, and with police and the media surrounding us, we celebrated communion.

Most of the police sat back and watched, not daring to arrest anyone, especially during communion. Then we continued the "breaking of the bread" by bringing in pizzas. It was a love feast, and then we slept overnight in the park with our homeless friends. We did that week after week, with the police watching over us and the media standing by. And then one night after worship as we slept under the "Love" sign, which we had covered with a big question mark, the police circled the park and arrested all of us.

As Claiborne stood before the judge, he wore a shirt that read, "Jesus was homeless." The judge was intrigued. He hadn't realized Jesus had been homeless.

After hearing the arguments, the judge decided that although laws had clearly been broken, the constitutionality of such laws was in question. He declared, "Let me remind the court that if it weren't for people who broke unjust laws, we wouldn't have the freedom that we have. We'd still have slavery. That's the story of this country, from the Boston Tea Party to the civil rights movement. These people are not criminals; they are freedom fighters. I find them all not guilty, on every charge."

The newspapers pronounced it a "Revolutionary Court Decision," and Claiborne claims that the judge asked him for a "Jesus was homeless" T-shirt.[1]

Of course, the sacrificial love shared in Philadelphia's Love Park didn't originate in the hearts of the citizens. It originated in God's heart. We are simply the vessels through which God expresses His love for the world—the whole world, not just the lovable in it or those who profess Him as their Lord and Savior. He loves every person who's ever walked the planet. Not only that, God loves Adolf Hitler as much as He loves Abraham or Aaron, He loves Jeffrey Dahmer no less than He loves David or Daniel, and He loves Saddam Hussein as much as He loves Sarah or Solomon.

Can we ever learn to love like that? Can we look beyond a person's failings and recognize their greatest need—to experience the life-transforming love of God? While showing such love may be life's greatest challenge, we can begin by simply loving those God has placed around us—both the lovable and unlovable.

HOLDING HIS HAND

Is loving others something I find easy or difficult? Why?

_____

_____

_____

How can I overcome any fear of negative consequences in order to show love to others? How can I deny myself in order to help someone else gain eternal life?

_____

_____

_____

Can I choose to love God but refuse to love others? If not, how can I love those who seem so unlovable?

_____

_____

_____

Loving Creator,

You showed us what true love is. You sent Your only Son to die, just so that we could spend eternity with You. Thank you for making such a huge sacrifice for our benefit. Now inspire us to overcome our fears of what love may cost us, for we have so much more to gain by showing Your love to others than by selfishly refusing to do so. In Jesus' name. Amen.

HAVE FAITH
IN THE UNSEEN

Daily reading: Hebrews 11:1–40

Key passage: What is faith? It is the confident assurance that what we hope for is going to happen. It is the evidence of things we cannot yet see. God gave his approval to people in days of old because of their faith. (Hebrews 11:1–2)

*Y*ears ago I heard a joke that has stuck with me. Sally's science teacher asks, "Do you see the window on that wall?"

"Yes," Sally replies.

"Do you see the tree outside that window?"

"Yes."

"Do you see the nest in that tree branch?"

"Yes," Sally replies a third time.

"Do you see God?" the teacher asks.

"No," says Sally.

"That's because God doesn't exist!" the teacher insists.

Sally then asked the class, "Do you see that desk in the front of the room?"

"Yes," the class responds.

"Do you see that teacher behind that desk?"

"Yes."

"Do you see that head on the teacher's body?"

"Yes," the class replies a third time.

"Do you see a brain in that head?"

"No," says the class.

"That's because it doesn't exist!" Sally exclaims.

It's not the best joke in the world, but it does make a very good point. Not all things that exist are visible to the human eye. I can't see the millions of bacteria on a public bathroom door handle at an airport or see the millions of germs flying through the atmosphere when someone sneezes on an airplane, but I know they exist when I get a sore throat or a runny nose after my trip. I've never seen a cold front, but when I leave my house in eighty-degree weather and return home that evening to forty-degree temperatures, I know that a cold front blew in. I can't see the sugar molecules in a slice of birthday cake and a glass of root beer, but let my son eat and drink them and I know he's on a big-time sugar buzz! There are lots of things we can't see with our eyes, yet we can still know they exist because of the effect they have in this world.

Faith in God is very much the same. We cannot visualize it with our eyes, but we can sense it in our spirits and demonstrate it to the world. The "great cloud of witnesses" (Hebrews 12:1, NIV) you read about today—ordinary people like Noah, Abraham and Sarah, Moses, Rahab, David, and many more—were heralded not for their fame, good looks, intelligence, charm, or fortunes. Scripture tells us God applauded the saints of old simply *because of their faith* (Hebrews 11:2, 39).

Although invisible to the human eye, faith is very visible to God. I believe it can also be visible to potential believers when they open the eyes of their hearts. I recently attended a funeral where a grieving widow stood and spoke of her husband's love for the Lord, explaining that her tears weren't for Stan, but for herself and her family because they would miss him. She proclaimed her knowledge that her husband was now in the presence of Jesus, and for that she was able to rejoice and anticipate their heavenly reunion someday. The stability in her voice and the peace of her countenance broadcast her rock-solid faith in God so that anyone who wasn't a believer surely walked out of that church wondering what they were missing.

I also heard a woman talk of how her husband of thirty years suddenly filed for divorce, leaving her with financial burdens far beyond what she could bear, especially with a mentally retarded child and an invalid mother living with her. In spite of these horrendous circumstances, this woman boldly declared, "But I know that God is with me through all of this! I can feel His presence and sense His peace like never before, and I have no doubt that He'll continue to care for my every need." If faith were apples, I could have plucked basketfuls from her every limb.

These women are radiant testimonies that a believer's faith is real, and Jesus' presence in our lives is undeniable. Even if we can't witness Him with our eyes, we can be a witness for Him so that the spiritual eyes of others can be opened.

If the Bible were still being written today, would our names be included in the great cloud of witnesses? Would God applaud us for having the kind of faith in Him that He longs for us to have? Will our faith withstand the future tests of time, trials, and tribulations? I pray that this five-book series has brought you to the point in your relationship with Christ where you can, without hesitation, answer these questions with a great big resounding, "Yes!"

If that is the case, I have no doubt you will continue drawing as many people into God's kingdom as possible, for as today's passage declared about the saints who've gone before us: "None of them received all that God had promised. For God had far better things in mind for us that would also benefit them, for they can't receive the prize at the end of the race until we finish the race" (Hebrews 11:39–40). So let's press on with our evangelistic efforts, for we all have a great reward in store for us when Jesus returns to collect His bride, and we get to feast together at the great wedding supper of the Lamb!

HOLDING HIS HAND

Do I believe that I am truly the bride of Christ? What evidence do I have that my faith is well placed?

_____

_____

_____

As I express my faith in things I can't see with my eyes, but know in my heart of hearts, what impact can I have on others? What am I doing (or will I commit to do) to draw others toward His extravagant love?

_____

_____

_____

> _Dearest Heavenly Bridegroom,_
>
> _We eagerly await Your return, Lord Jesus, and greatly anticipate spending eternity in Your loving presence! Make us completely irresistible to others, so that they will catch the spiritual bouquet and be drawn into an intimate love relationship with You as well! Amen._

THE END...OR JUST
THE BEGINNING?

I am so proud of you for diving so deeply into God's Word throughout these five books! As you reach the closing of this last devotional in the Loving Jesus Without Limits series, ask yourself: Is this the end? Or could it be just the beginning—the beginning of a continuous intimate walk with my precious heavenly Bridegroom? I pray it is the latter, and that these books have set the stage for you to enjoy basking in His presence every day of your life.

While you may not be able to see the impact these daily readings have made on you, God certainly can. Even though you've turned every page, the journey is not yet over. My prayer is that you will continue to study God's Word and let Him do all He wants to do in you to transform you into His likeness. I pray you will be able to continue relating with Him so intimately that the evidence of your spiritual growth and maturity will be undeniable to all who know you. I pray you will continue to have faith, especially in the things you cannot see with your human eyes. For it is true that...

- We cannot see Jesus preparing the heavenly wedding chamber for His beloved bride, but we can know for certain that we'll spend eternity with Him someday.
- We cannot see God's love, but we can be absolutely overwhelmed by it when we recognize His passionate pursuit of us.
- We cannot see His forgiveness, but we can feel it in every fiber of our being as we respond to God's transforming grace with confidence.
- We are unable to lay eyes upon many of His spiritual blessings, but we can continue unwrapping God's extraordinary gifts to us every day of our lives.

- We cannot recognize how irresistible our passionate relationship with God may be to others, but we can confidently attempt to draw them toward His extravagant love as well.

Will you join me in continuing to strive to be completely His? Let's continue to learn more and more about how we can grow to love Jesus without any limits at all.

A NOTE FROM SHANNON

Are you looking for a unique idea for a women's retreat? An extraordinary experience for women of all ages, from all walks of life to drive home the encouraging principles presented in this book? Consider hosting a Completely His event that allows women to experience the joy of committing their "bridal love" to Jesus Christ, their heavenly Bridegroom.

Because a bride doesn't feel like a bride until she walks down the aisle wearing white, this event resembles a wedding ceremony in many ways, and yet is unlike any other—a sweet foretaste of the great wedding supper of the Lamb that is yet to come for all of us someday!

My ministry assistants and I have coordinated these events the past several years for groups as small as ten and as large as four hundred. Participants describe the experience as "powerfully real" (Lyn, age 52), incomparable ("no wedding will ever compare," Tracy, age 20), and "life transforming" (Samantha, age 38).

Go to www.shannonethridge.com for plenty of creative ideas, DVDs, and other products, as well as downloadable forms to help you coordinate your own Completely His women's event.

Notes

Day 2

1. Hardy, Barbara, "Towards a Poetics of Fiction: An Approach through Narrative," *Novel: A Forum on Fiction*, 2, (Fall, 1968): 5. www.edst.educ .ubc.ca/aerc/2000/normanr-web.htm.
2. Jimmy Carter, *Sources of Strength: Meditations on Scripture for a Living Faith* (New York: Times Books, 1997), 71–72.
3. Carter, *Sources of Strength*, 72.

Day 4

1. Verena Dobnik, "NYC Subway Savior Showered with Gifts," Associated Press, January 4, 2007. www.sfgate.com/cgi-bin/ article.cgi?f=/n/a/2007/ 01/04/national/a162834S90.DTL and Jill Gardiner, "Subway Hero Gets the Red Carpet Treatment," *The New York Sun*, January 5, 2007. www.nysun.com/article/ 46140?page_no=1.

Day 9

1. "Paul, the Apostle," iLumina Bible Software, Tyndale, 2003.
2. Jessica McCaleb, "Blogging Teens," *World*, September 16, 2006, 34–35. Submitted by Brittany Tarr, Wheaton, Illinois. www.preachingtoday .com/illustrations/article_print.html?id=39330.

Day 11

1. Kenneth L. Barker and John R. Kohlenberger III, *The Expositor's Bible Commentary*, Abridged Edition: New Testament (Grand Rapids, MI: Zondervan, 1994), 470–71.

Day 13

1. Susan Duke, *Earth Angels* (West Monroe, LA: Howard, 2002), 90–91.

Day 18

1. Jim Yardley, " 'Guardian Angel' Patrols Suicide Bridge," New York Times News Service, *Chicago Tribune*, September 21, 2004. Submitted by Lee Eclov, Vernon Hills, Illinois. www.preachingtoday.com/illustrations/article_print.html?id=26066.

Day 19

1. "Silas," iLumina Bible Software, Tyndale, 2003.
2. "Silas," iLumina Bible Software.
3. Ron Wilson, "10-year-old Raises $43,000 for Habitat for Humanity," *San Antonio Express-News*, August 5, 2006. www.mysanantonio.com/news/metro/stories/MYSA080506.01A.habitat_hero.1ebb4.

Day 23

1. Nicholas Kristof, "Bargaining for Freedom," NYTimes.com. www.nytimes.com/2004/01/21/opinion/21KRIS.html?ex=1390021200&en=103bf815.
2. www.preachingtoday.com/25540; submitted by Aaron Goerner, Utica, New York.

Day 24

1. "Facts About Hunger," www.youthnoise.com/page.php?page_id=422.
2. www.youthnoise.com/page.php?page_id=422.
3. www.youthnoise.com/page.php?page_id=504.

Day 25

1. This was not always the case. Joseph was assigned as captain of the palace guard and served in Potiphar's house without being castrated.

2. "Eunuch," iLumina Bible Software, Tyndale, 2003.

3. Kenneth L. Barker and John R. Kohlenberger III, *The Expositor's Bible Commentary*, Abridged Edition: New Testament (Grand Rapids, MI: Zondervan, 1994), 428–29.

Day 26

1. Hal Karp, "Roadside E.R.," *Reader's Digest*, August 2006. www.rd.com/content/openContent.do?contentId=32012.

Day 27

1. Philip Yancey, *What's So Amazing About Grace?* (Grand Rapids, MI: Zondervan, 1997), 208.

Day 28

1. Kevin G. Harney, *Seismic Shifts* (Grand Rapids, MI: Zondervan, 2005), 200.

Day 29

1. Shane Claiborne, *The Irresistible Revolution* (Grand Rapids, MI: Zondervan, 2006), 232–36.

Topical Index

SCRIPTURE INDEX